LEGACY
Leadership

LEGACY Leadership

Growing Your Most Valuable Resource: Your People

Chris Ross

Published by Game Changer Publishing

Paperback ISBN: 978-1-964811-16-1
Hardcover ISBN: 978-1-964811-17-8
Digital ISBN: 978-1-964811-18-5

www.GameChangerPublishing.com

DEDICATION

To my children, Jayden, Ilana, and Everly, my goal in this life is to create a man that you are proud to call your Dad and for each of you to realize your truest potential. The three of you embody the best parts of me. I cherish and love every moment I get to spend exploring life with you.

To my incredible wife, Cathy, you have taught me more about life and leadership than anyone. Your commitment to our family and marriage inspires me to become more, do more, and grow more. Thank you for always believing in me and never allowing my craziness to change your heart.

I love you more than you'll ever know. I plan to spend the rest of my energy trying to prove it!

Read This First

Just to say thanks for buying and reading my book, I would like to give you a free collaboration call with me, no strings attached!

Scan the QR Code Here:

LEGACY Leadership

Growing Your Most Valuable Resource:

Your People

Chris Ross

www.GameChangerPublishing.com

Praise for LEGACY Leadership

"*LEGACY Leadership* is a compelling and enlightening read that offers an actionable roadmap to achieving excellence in leadership. Chris masterfully delivers keen insights into how leaders can rise to the occasion when facing challenging situations. Through vivid examples, he illustrates how effective leadership can transform obstacles into opportunities, serving as powerful motivators and reminders that with the right mindset and strategies, extraordinary accomplishments are within reach.

This book is essential for anyone looking to elevate their leadership skills with proven insights. Whether you are a seasoned leader or an aspiring one, Chris's guidance will equip you with the tools and knowledge necessary to enhance your leadership capabilities. *LEGACY Leadership* is a must-read for those seeking to understand the dynamics of effective leadership and the importance of self-growth, transparency, and discipline in leading teams to success."

– **Susan Norris, PhD, Chief Executive Officer, Deer Oaks Behavioral Health**

"The depth of understanding and practical wisdom shared throughout the book is remarkable. Chris masterfully addresses the critical elements of effective communication, including empathy, clarity, and cultural sensitivity, providing readers with valuable strategies to enhance their interactions with patients, families, and colleagues. The real-world scenarios and case studies included are particularly impactful, offering concrete examples that illustrate the application of these communication principles in everyday situations. The author's expertise and dedication to improving post-acute care are evident and deeply appreciated."

– **Nicole Kaufman, Chief Transformation Officer, Genesis Healthcare**

Foreword

Effective leadership is an essential differentiator that spells success or failure in business.

Anyone with even minimal experience in the business world understands this as a simple but powerful fact. However, it's a topic that is both easily understood but challenging to master for many people. That's because blending universal core leadership principles with an individual interpretation of how to apply them is unique to each person.

We know a lot about leadership, but like a proverbial moving target, there's still much for us to learn. That's why I highly recommend that you read *LEGACY Leadership*.

In this book, my friend Chris Ross explores what it takes to be a great leader based on his considerable success and meteoric rise as a top-flight sales executive in the healthcare industry. Shaped by his experiences as an employee and as the CEO of his own company, Legacy Healthcare Consulting, Chris has distilled several essential and transportable lessons about how to lead others effectively.

As you'll learn, Chris works from the premise that leadership is a skill and not a trait, and learning leadership skills are teachable but perishable. Like any skill, you must use that knowledge daily to remain effective as a leader. Otherwise, you risk losing your edge and the ability to optimally lead others for the benefit of everyone in your organization.

This is enhanced by Chris's belief that people are every organization's most valuable resource. It's no secret that when you pay close attention to your most valuable resource and help them to grow, you become a leader that other talented people gravitate to, creating a culture with exponential potential. Using his Pillars of Performance, Chris also explores why leaders must integrate an emphasis on people with a clear understanding of process, product, and plan to help them effectively lead with empathy and grace.

Throughout his journey, I have been impressed by Chris's ability to distill and analyze important information and convey it with clear and concise communication. He has used that talent to create an enviable and compassionate track record of success that is now well-documented in *LEGACY Leadership*.

Chris is fully engaged in his career, but one of the things I also admire most about him is that he places a high priority on his family life. Balancing his duties as a CEO and a loving husband and father creates a higher purpose that feeds his daily efforts to lead others. He is more than just a role model for effective business leadership; he is a role model for how to live a purpose-driven life in all areas.

As you read *LEGACY Leadership*, remember it's one thing to assemble the right team with the right mission aligned with the same standards and goals. It's quite another to lead that team daily and produce results and success that everyone can share.

If you agree with that kind of thinking—and you should—*LEGACY Leadership* is an insightful must-read with important strategies you can put to work today and for the rest of your life.

– Ben Newman
USA Today TOP 5 Mindset & Performance Coach
2x Wall Street Journal Bestseller

Table of Contents

Introduction 1

A LEGACY Leader... 7

...Uses the Pillars of Performance as a Guide 7

...Listens, Learns, and Leads by Example 19

...Leads with Empathy 27

...Extends Grace 37

...Practices Compassionate Accountability 51

...Utilizes Communication as the Foundation for Growth 65

...Grows Themselves in Order to Grow Others 75

...Positively Impacts Culture 89

Conclusion 97

Introduction

As far back as I can remember, I have always dreamed of being a healthcare professional. Growing up in poverty and not having many role models when I was young, I was always fascinated by doctors and dentists. I thought they were all wealthy, successful, and happy—everything I wanted to be. My mother made most of our Halloween costumes when I was a child. Year after year, I'd don my oversized green scrubs and surgical mask, which I'm fairly sure my mother acquired during a hospital visit—presumably without the permission of said hospital. Growing up, I had a crooked smile, and my two front teeth were aggressively chipped as a result of fighting and football (two of my favorite pastimes as a kid). I was always aware of how that changed my face, so I became obsessed with the idea of becoming a dentist. I wanted to fix the smile of every poor kid in the country whose parents could not afford proper dental treatment. I grew up and never got around to medical or dental school, but that burning desire to be a part of the healthcare field never cooled off.

My healthcare journey started when I joined the United States Army as a Combat Medic. My military experience was deeply rewarding, and I am incredibly grateful for the lessons I learned and the relationships I was able to build, none more important or impressive than that with my wife. Our relationship started with her teaching me how to be a better medic. Some 18 years and three amazing children later, she spends every day teaching me how to be a better man. I spent my first three years of active duty training and working on a Medical-Surgical unit at Brooke Army Medical Center in San Antonio, Texas. My deployment to Baghdad, Iraq, in support of Operation Iraqi Freedom, gave me a new perspective on life and death. I was fortunate to be part of the Emergency Room team at Ibn Sina Hospital in the heart of Baghdad at the height of the war from 2005 to 2006. We had a 96% survival rate of injured Americans, an accomplishment that remains near the top of my "Things to Be Proud Of" list to this day.

This deployment gave me the opportunity to learn more about the bedside aspects of healthcare, with real-world experience and a front-row seat to all the elements that war and injury bring to humans, soldiers, civilians, and even enemy combatants. These events only confirmed what I innately understood as a child: Healthcare is where I am supposed to be. As I transitioned out of the Army, I went back to school, intending to become a physician. But those plans changed when I found out I was going to be a father. It was time to make a little money!

Medical supply sales seemed like a natural path. I was comfortable with the products and have always been blessed with the gift of gab. During that time, I was exposed to post-acute care simply by calling on skilled nursing facilities while attempting to acquire them as customers. However, one facility drew me in: Cedarwood Health Care Center in Colorado Springs, Colorado. I continued to visit even though they weren't buying anything. From the first time we met, I had a great connection with the administrator.

One day, she asked a question that would forever change the fabric of my being, help me discover my professional purpose, and set me on a journey that I am still on 15-plus years later. She asked if I had ever thought about getting into sales in post-acute care, specifically about being her sales professional. I wasn't exactly sure what that meant. I didn't understand the intricacies of a sales professional in post-acute care. I had no clue about the journey I was about to start when I agreed to join her team as a clinical liaison.

Cedarwood was the bottom performer in a large national portfolio at the time. The team assembled was about to do something extraordinary. We came together and focused on quality and customer service. I concentrated on telling our story to anyone who would listen. I joined the team in May. At that time, they had admitted eight residents the entire year. At the end of my second week there, we admitted eight residents—on a Friday! I was really popular with the nursing staff—about as popular as Seahawks coach Pete Carroll was in Seattle when he decided to pass the ball on the 1-yard line, a decision that led to Tom Brady and the Patriots earning their fourth Super Bowl Championship. We continued to experience success and growth that year and were the top-performing facility in the portfolio for several months.

Due to our performance and the team's support at Cedarwood, I was able to rise through the sales ranks of the organization. In approximately 18 months, I became a Regional Sales Manager (RSM). During my tenure as an RSM, our region never fell below number two in the organization, which operated around 200 homes nationwide. I am still good friends with the RSM who continued to push and challenge me for the top spot. Due to our performance, I was fortunate enough to be selected to become part of the most elite sales team in the organization, the Strengths, Weaknesses, Opportunities, Threats (SWOT) Team.

Outside of owning my own company, my role on the SWOT Team is absolutely my favorite professional experience. We were sent to bottom-performing homes across the country for 8-week assignments to assess, diagnose, and fix anything that was preventing the home from being successful. Our outcomes were measured on the speed of effectiveness and sustainability. Through relentless effort and hard work, I was the #1 Executive Director of Business Development on the SWOT Team for the duration of my time there. While being #1 has always been my goal, the truest measurement of success during that time was that different leaders throughout the organization were requesting me to be assigned to their divisions, regions, or homes. This is a team that was generally avoided due to the nature of our role, so to be requested was a huge compliment and really solidified my understanding of the importance of collaboration over control. Due to my success on the SWOT Team, I earned the opportunity to become the Division Vice President of Sales over the entire western part of the United States, which at its height included responsibility for more than 60 homes across four time zones.

Throughout my time with this organization, I was part of a team with the number one building at the liaison level, the number one region, the number one division, and the number one Executive Director on the most elite sales team. I attribute all of that success to my unrelenting desire to learn and my obsession with collaboration. I have found that if you approach a challenge with an open mind and heart, the possibilities are truly endless. Beyond that, I was able to serve as the Senior Vice President of Sales and the Chief Marketing Officer at several large regional and national organizations across the country.

After years of leading sales professionals and being fortunate enough to work with amazing operators and clinicians who were always willing to teach, I felt it was time to start something I could call my own. In 2018, I founded Legacy Healthcare Consulting with the simple mission of *Improving Quality through Collaboration.* I wanted to focus on improving our care setting. I believed the most effective way to do that was to start an organization founded on quality and built on collaboration.

As we embarked on the journey of writing this book, we reflected extensively on our real-world experience and the methods we have developed, executed, and proven in today's chaotic environment. We've created methods that are easy to understand, simple to implement (but not necessarily easy), and, most importantly, sustainable. Full disclaimer: While the concepts in the book are proven, they are also proven to take time, commitment, and continued effort. We do not have a quick fix. It also takes a great deal of consistency. As with anything worthwhile, you must remain consistent with your leadership practice. You can't try it for a week and expect results. You must develop a leadership style composed of these elements while adapting each of them to your unique personality and the needs of those in your care.

We firmly believe that leadership is a skill, not a trait. Skills can be taught and learned. Skills are also perishable. These characteristics describe leadership perfectly. Like any skill, you will lose it if you do not use it. The following chapters will focus on the LEGACY Leadership process, which, when executed properly, will positively influence your most valuable resource: your people. We believe that post-acute care leaders have a significant need for resources that can help them grow and develop as leaders. While there are countless books on leadership, few, if any, are written by someone with applicable knowledge and experience in post-acute care. We care about post-acute leaders in part because we are post-acute leaders. We believe the only way to improve our care setting is to grow our people, which starts and ends with leadership. Our goal is to make a significant positive difference in the lives of our residents and staff and enhance the reputation of post-acute care as a whole. We are convinced this is the best way to accomplish that.

As we have shared, our mission is to *Improve Quality through Collaboration*. This book represents our attempt to collaborate with as many leaders as possible and share ideas, resources, and lessons learned. The aging population across the country is growing daily. Turnover and burnout of employees in post-acute care are at an all-time high. The regulatory environment is more intense than ever, and it's going to get tougher. Relationships between operators, clinicians, government entities, and payers continue to be stressed. Margins are extremely thin. Experienced leaders are retiring; young leaders need more direction and guidance. The post-acute work environment and workforce needs are shifting. The use of technology and automation is growing. Younger people want to be grown and led. The new workforce and future leaders will change employers and careers if those needs are not met. Society is finally starting to focus on purpose and fulfillment. If your leadership style does not foster an environment where your people have the autonomy to grow, discover their purpose, and fulfill it, you will constantly be at risk of losing them.

At Legacy, we created a process that can be widely shared and implemented. We freely share information, resources, and relationships. We work every day to live the LEGACY Leadership process internally and externally. We believe in these principles and believe the solution to improving post-acute care lies with the individual leaders: you. We feel that as the individual leaders grow and improve their skill sets, we will collectively grow and improve our care setting. The fact that you have opened this book tells us that you desire to be part of the solution, and that is enough for us to welcome you to the Legacy family. We are excited and grateful to play a small role in your growth as a leader. Thank you for joining us on this journey. We hope you enjoy it as much as we do.

A LEGACY Leader...

...Uses the Pillars of Performance as a Guide

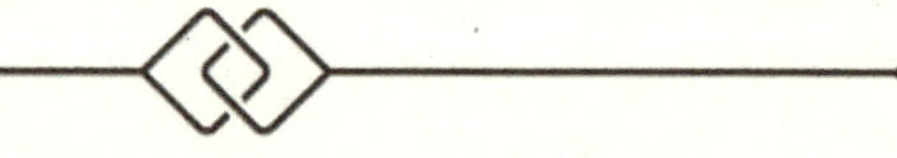

The Legacy Pillars of Performance provide the framework for everything we do. From our internal communication and strategic development to our client selection, we use our Pillars to guide 100% of our decisions and direction. Leadership is no exception: We use our Pillars of Performance as the framework for our LEGACY Leadership model. At this stage, we'll cover the Pillars so that you understand the value of each one and how they individually contribute to the overall model. We find it impossible to experience sustainable success with the absence of any one of the Pillars, so they are all equally valuable, and each is absolutely necessary.

The Legacy Pillars of Performance are People, Process, Product, and Plan.

As with everything we do, we will start with our most valuable resource: people. When you put people first, everything becomes clear.

The First Pillar: People

Countless stories are told every day that highlight the importance of putting your people first and truly valuing the human capital that comprises your team. I have personally experienced both ends of this spectrum. I have been part of a team that put people over everything, and as a result, people grew, and the team won. I have also been part of a team that valued profitability over people. Unfortunately—but not surprisingly—those teams and managers do not last long.

One of my experiences highlights both sides of this coin. I was collaborating with a skilled nursing facility, where there was a great Executive Director who cared tremendously about their people. They led the facility exceptionally well. They focused on quality. They focused on bringing people together, highlighting their strengths, improving their weaknesses as a team, and working together. The team responded exceptionally well to their leader. This young, ambitious leader built a strong team of department heads that focused on improving quality and collaborating to support one another with their residents' needs at the center of every decision.

Over a short period of time, the home started to improve its overall quality, and it became a destination where people wanted to receive care. The home was soon full, 100% occupied, which is an incredible feat in itself. In addition to being fully occupied, the team made it a priority to focus on quality and regulatory compliance. During an annual survey visit, they received a deficiency-free survey, which was another impressive accomplishment in the competitive environment and market in which they operated. As a result of their flawless survey, their overall star rating continued to improve, and they eventually achieved the coveted five-star status.

The leader believed in their people, valued them, challenged them, grew them, and most importantly, supported them to accomplish their mission. This team's success not only impacted the team members positively but also affected the residents and family members who were fortunate enough to call this place home. Unfortunately, this good thing came to an end—or perhaps just a pause.

This administrator then had an opportunity to grow outside of this organization, and they took a higher role with a competitor. They left, and things began to change almost immediately. On paper, the only thing that changed was the leader. But in reality, what fundamentally changed everything was how the leader made the people feel. The leader changed, and quality followed. All of the value created by the team started to erode because the new leader was not pouring value into the people.

The home that was once full, with a waiting list, fell below 70% occupancy, and they ran into regulatory trouble. When your people do not feel supported or empowered, it shows in their work. In this particular home, the quality of care and care delivery suffered the most. The home received multiple high-scope and severity violations with significant fines attached. Reputation suffered, census suffered, and revenues suffered. The catalyst for this cascade of adverse outcomes was the change in leadership and the loss of one simple quality: caring about people.

Fortunately for this home and team, the former administrator ended up returning to the home. While it has not been easy, the leader knew the play that needed to be run: Take care of the people, and they will take care of the business.

Today, the building is consistently occupied at over 95% capacity, and on many days, it is completely full. They are fully staffed with their own employees and do not have to rely on agency staff to fill any positions or shifts. They recently had a deficiency-free survey and are on their way back to achieving their five-star overall status. The one thing that changed was the leader, the person that put people first.

This story highlights the critical importance of putting people first, as we understand they are our most valuable resource. You want to make your people feel heard: Listen to them. You want to build trust with them: Follow through on what you say you're going to do. Be an honest leader and invest selflessly in your people, and you'll create an environment where there's inspiration and aspiration. You are responsible for building that environment through communication, trust, and action. When you have a mentality of people over profits, your productivity and profitability will grow just as your people do. Grow your people and give them the autonomy to grow your profits. When you get the people right, everything becomes a little bit simpler. It's not easy, but it is simple. If people are wrong, nothing else matters. You can't outwork a bad team; you need to fix the team first. No other solution or strategy is sustainable. You can experience some success, and you may force some business growth, but you will not be able to sustain any level of success unless you focus on and support your people.

Another important element about people is that this process never ends. There is no finish line because you constantly try to grow and improve your people. Improve the support you give them and improve their environment so they can improve your product. At Legacy, we focus a tremendous amount of our energy and efforts on our people and encourage our clients to do the same. No surprise here, but as we get into the LEGACY Leadership model, it will be all about how to grow and lead your people.

As you get the people figured out, you feel like you have the right team assembled, and everyone clearly understands their roles & responsibilities. The next step is for your people to start focusing on our second Pillar, your product.

The Second Pillar: Product

When your people are focused on the quality of your product and improving it over time, that will lead you to discover sustainable solutions that match perfectly with the needs of your market. When I first started in post-acute care, I was at a small facility on the southwest side of Colorado Springs. It was an old, dilapidated building that was battleship gray with Christmas tree green trim around the outside. During my second week at the facility, there were police cars and a news crew across the street dealing with a problem at a house in the neighborhood. Our administrator had to go outside to request the news crew not to get our sign in their shot. We were not in the greatest area, didn't have the greatest product, didn't have the greatest reputation, and didn't need that type of publicity. Many of our residents had a diagnosis of a major mental illness, which caused multiple challenges with our regulatory environment, the quality of care we were able to provide, and the quality of referrals that we were able to receive from our various referral sources. It was part of an organization that operated 185 homes, and this home was number 185 in the rankings. The home had many opportunities for improvement and rightfully earned the reputation as a bottom feeder in the Colorado Springs market. It was a challenging product. The team did not do a lot of things well, and the reputation was understandably damaged.

Fortunately, I was able to join the team at a time when the leader was somebody who cared about people. They had recently built a team of leaders in each department who were great at what they did, had an exceptional skill set, cared about the product, and cared about the people in their care. As a result, the team focused on creating a high-quality product, improving each other, and producing sustainable plans that would last beyond the length of a stay for a single resident. They all worked diligently to ensure that the experience of every resident, family member, staff member, and vendor was a positive one.

After a few months of being with this team and understanding their goal, I was able to contribute by bringing them higher-quality referrals and converting many of those into admissions. Our outlook on admissions had changed. We put in tremendous effort to ensure we could effectively meet the needs of each resident. This approach created a great deal of pride among the staff. They no longer felt like a "dumping ground." The team was proud of the care they were able to provide and worked hard to create success stories, which I would proudly share with our community to highlight all of their hard work. As their sales professional, I was able to use these success stories to demonstrate to the market how much the product had changed. We started at the bottom as a one-star facility with a bad reputation in a challenging neighborhood. The neighborhood did not change, but as we focused on the product, our reputation and star rating started to rise. When the right team focused on the quality of the product, the product improved. We raised our overall star rating to four stars.

You need to focus on the quality of your product. You have to have a team that cares. Quality is the vehicle that will take you to your destination, good or bad. You cannot outsell a bad product if you want to create long-term, sustainable success. A great product or service will create positive word of mouth, and the opposite is also true. A good product will make it very easy to sell. I benefited from a good product in Colorado Springs. It made the job of selling that product much easier. We received a higher volume of referrals and higher quality referrals, and we were, therefore, able to select the referrals that allowed us to grow our product and become a better resource to our community. A poor product will lead to unhappy employees and unhappy customers.

The most challenging part of creating a good product is time. We have countless competing priorities in our care setting. You will never find the perfect time—you need to make time. You have to make time for the things that matter the most, and focusing on your product is one of them. Any other approach is temporary and unsustainable. So you have to choose whether you're going to make time to focus on your product and improve the quality or you're going to make excuses and continue to regress. As we begin to focus on our product, we need clear direction as to where to focus, what to do, who's responsible, and how we're going to accomplish this together. In order to do this effectively, you have to have a solid process, which is our third pillar.

The Third Pillar: Process

Regarding the process, you must have a clearly defined method for achieving your goals. You have to set standards that will get you to the destination you want. During my time with a large national post-acute operator, we didn't always have the best product. In certain markets, we didn't even have the best people. But we always had really solid processes that allowed us to compensate for our shortcomings and buy time to fix the other areas (to fix the people and the product). The organization had many solid processes, some of which I still utilize today. The process I was most involved in and most familiar with was our sequential sales model. The sequential structure allowed us to know exactly where we were in the sales process at all times. It also allowed us to communicate effectively with our referral sources, facility leadership, and future residents.

When we implemented and executed consistently, our sales process allowed us to generate more referrals, convert more referrals into admissions, and work with our clinical leaders to plan discharges appropriately. All of these elements contributed to census growth, regardless of the market or the overall star rating in various homes. Our process allowed us to transcend some of the limitations that would otherwise slow or prevent our success. It also allowed us time to fix those limitations and fix the product. We could buy time by following a solid process that allowed us to compensate for the other areas.

Processes are incredibly important. This is the reason we created the LEGACY Leadership model as a process. We want to give you clear direction, make sure you understand where you are in the process, and ensure you're able to communicate with those that you're trying to lead so that everybody's on the same page. We have worked to build clear, concise, and applicable processes to encourage consistency among our clients and, now, among our readers too. We want to make it as simple as possible, as simplicity allows for adoption and application. In addition, we wanted to create a process that allows for autonomy.

Picture yourself on a journey. You are headed to New York, and you want to be there by the fifteenth of the month. That's the only direction you have: Get to New York by the fifteenth. How you get there—whether you drive, fly, run, swim, or take a hot air balloon—that's up to you. The mile markers along the way will let you know if you're headed in the right direction. You can make adjustments along the way; you can speed up or slow down. You have the autonomy to choose your mode of transportation and the route that you take. A solid process will allow for independence so that you have some choice along the way in how you get there, but we do not change the destination.

On this trip, we must also consider adverse events like a flat tire or a canceled flight. Flexibility is key because we are making it to New York by the fifteenth. Great leaders are flexible with their methods and rigid with their standards. A solid process will ensure your team is able to meet your standards, but how those standards are met is completely up to your people. This autonomy will inspire innovation and creativity among the team. The best leaders create thinkers and problem-solvers, not robots and certainly not mindless followers.

Documentation is also vital in processes. In healthcare, we all understand that documentation is crucial. You have to document this journey. You have to document your process. You have to write down where you started and where you're going so that you can self-assess along the way and celebrate successes. You can reflect as things move forward, as you work on growing your people, improving your product, and refining your process. You can identify adjustments needed through documentation. It allows you to reflect on how far you've come, and very importantly, it ensures that the team is all on the same page. Documentation is a valuable part of any process, and we all understand that if it isn't documented, it didn't happen.

The Fourth Pillar: Plan

When you combine great people, a quality product, and a solid process, you create an effective plan, whether it's a sales plan, a business plan, or a leadership plan. A well-crafted plan serves as a crucial reference point, showing our progress, current position, and intended direction. Our plan not only guides us but also acts as an official record. Documenting your strategy is essential because a goal without a plan is merely a dream, and dreams don't become reality without a plan and hard work. While hope is an inspiring feeling, it is not a viable strategy. So, make sure to build and document your plan!

As I started in post-acute care, I was extremely focused on my sales plan. As a sales professional, I had tremendous pride in my role and felt a sense of responsibility to create a solid plan to share with the team. Each week, I would meet with my home's leadership team, and before our weekly meetings, I would build a sales plan. I would prepare for this meeting by creating a plan for my activity throughout the week. I would focus on market intel, census data, scheduled meetings, marketing opportunities, and service calls for existing referral sources. I was always prepared for this meeting. It was the one time each week we were going to discuss business development, which was my favorite topic at the time.

As I laid out my plan for the leadership team, we had open dialogue and discussion about all business development opportunities. I welcomed constructive criticism and tried to ensure all of my planned activity was supported by data and market intelligence. Together, we would create a commitment to what our census was going to be at the end of the week. "Commitment" is the key word in that sentence because we were not making a guess. We were not hoping to achieve a number. We were absolutely committed to achieving that number and doing whatever was required to make that happen. This approach allowed everyone to have an opportunity to contribute to the plan. We would discuss how each department could contribute to our census goals. While I was the sales professional and ultimately had to answer for the census numbers, there were other team members who could contribute.

The nursing department was able to help prevent residents from returning to the hospitals by discharging inappropriately. The social services department could help effectively plan discharges and communicate those plans to the team so we could all help the resident transition back to the community successfully. My contribution was to generate more quality referrals and, through my process, to convert more of those referrals into admissions. By the end of each week's meeting, we transformed the plan from "my plan" to "our plan." This process of building a plan created buy-in, support, trust, grace, and, maybe most importantly, confidence among the team. We all stacked hands and agreed that this was the plan that was going to help us achieve our commitment.

Everyone understood their role and responsibilities and their required contributions to the plan, making the work more satisfying and our team much more successful. Through consistent efforts, we took this building from number 185 out of 185 to number 1 on a census and revenue measurement line. We were *extremely* successful. It was partly because we had a well-thought-out and well-documented plan. We had great people focused on improving the quality of our product, following a well-defined process, and creating a plan that we all agreed on, had confidence in, and could contribute to. We weren't successful every single week. There were times when we stumbled, there were times when we failed, but we were in it together. We could pivot easily because we had a well-documented plan; we would track our outcomes and adjust after a bad week. Those adjustments would prevent a bad week from turning into a bad month, and as a result, we continued our positive momentum until we reached the top of that mountain.

To achieve success, a team must have great people, a quality product, a proven process, and the ability to create and execute an effective plan. Clear communication about the ideal future state is essential, enabling everyone to understand the goals and how they can contribute to accomplishing them.

Having a plan is crucial, but it's important to understand that no plan is perfect. Plans should be built with flexibility in mind, allowing for adjustments as needed. Waiting for the perfect plan is a surefire way to fail; starting with an imperfect plan is better than nothing at all.

Execution is the key to success. Perfection is the enemy of progress and can prevent you from achieving your goals. Conditions will never be perfect, but you must have the courage to take action anyway. Courage is created through action, and the answers you seek lie on the other side of the struggle.

As you work through your plan, remember that failure is not final; it's simply feedback. Failing forward and learning from mistakes is part of the process. The people who have achieved high levels of success have likely failed more times than you have even attempted. Embrace failure as an opportunity to learn valuable lessons and continue striving for success.

Teams can overcome challenges and achieve their goals by focusing on clear communication, flexible planning, courageous execution, and learning from failure.

One of the most important elements of a solid plan is deleting the inessential. Removing the things that aren't required is critical. Great leaders inspire contributions from multiple team members. A strong plan is collaborative and not prescriptive. The more collaborative your plan is, the more buy-in you'll have and the more you will accomplish. People will work harder to ensure that their ideas do not fail.

Finally, after you build a solid plan and execute it, ensure that you have an after-action review period where the team can discuss lessons learned, pivots needed, and how to duplicate success. The most important element of the after-action review is understanding *why* you were successful and understanding what worked. If you cannot answer *why* you experienced success or *why* the plan worked, then you are simply lucky, and you can't duplicate or sustain luck. So make sure you understand the elements that have made you successful in order to be able to duplicate those and make them sustainable.

The LEGACY Model

Combining our people, product, process, and plan allows us to build a very successful leadership model. Our Pillars of Performance are the foundation that led us to the LEGACY Leadership model. LEGACY stands for:

L: Listen, Learn, & Lead by example

E: Empathy

G: Grace

A: Accountability

C: Communication

Y: You

Through this book, we're going to dive into each of these elements. We will discuss how you can improve in these areas to become a successful leader who puts people over profits and creates a quality product and a sustainable outcome so that your people are motivated, inspired, and excited to improve the post-acute care setting. We will also discuss the benefits of adopting a leadership model and the risks of ignoring the need for your people to be led. *Listening, Learning,* and *Leading* by example are all components of our L-phase. Let's take a closer look at how each component is necessary for a well-rounded leader.

A LEGACY Leader...

...Listens, Learns, and Leads by Example

As we built our model, we could not decide on a single word or phrase for the "L" in LEGACY, so we decided to include three: **Listen, Learn**, and **Lead** by example. We could not eliminate any of these elements without negatively impacting the overall LEGACY leadership model. All are critically and equally important. Let's start with the first: the ability to listen and truly understand what your team needs.

Listen

You have to listen with the intention to seek understanding. Many times, as leaders, while someone is discussing their challenges with us, we let our minds wander to think about solving those problems. We have to stay present in the moment and listen with the intention of seeking understanding so we can work through the solutions together. We will cover communication later in the process, but the first part of effective communication is hearing what your team has to say. You must remove all filters and any bias to clearly understand what they need from you as their leader.

Refrain from labeling information as good or bad; it simply is. The "good" lies in the fact that they're actually bringing you their challenges. They are communicating with you because they believe you care. They believe you can help them. In bringing you their problems, they demonstrate their confidence that you are a leader who will guide them towards solutions. Anytime your team stops bringing you their challenges, they've lost faith.

They either believe you and don't care, or you're unable to solve their problems. Either of these indicates a failure of leadership. You have to make sure that you are a talented listener in order to be a strong leader.

I had the opportunity to collaborate with a challenging facility that was on the special focus list in their state and had been on that dreaded list for some time. As I begin any collaborative effort, I schedule a set of one-on-one interviews with all the department heads to understand what they believe are the *Strengths, Weaknesses, Opportunities,* and *Threats* that exist within and outside of their home. I practiced and refined this very effective technique during my time on the SWOT Team.

I met with the director of nursing. She was incredibly talented and passionate about her home and her residents. She had phenomenal answers and very thoughtful ideas about each of the categories I covered. She clearly understood the strengths, weaknesses, opportunities, and threats of her home, team, and market. I asked her why she wasn't implementing these ideas or correcting any of the issues that had caused the trouble. Her answer was simple yet profound: She never felt heard, and this caused her to believe that the leadership team didn't want to listen to her ideas, so she stopped bringing them forward. The leadership of this home was not hearing their people. This leadership team was sitting on an employee who had answers, who had solutions, who wanted to do things to improve the quality of care they were providing and help the home evolve to ensure that they got off the special focus list and started to experience success again. They were ignoring all of that by simply not listening. We have to listen to our people to discover solutions.

Learn

As a leader, it's not your job to have all the answers. It's your responsibility to create an environment where the people with the answers want to share. You need to let go of the idea that leaders have the answers.

The most effective way to do that is to commit to being a lifelong learner. Helpfully, the post-acute care setting creates an environment where it is nearly impossible to think you know everything because our environment changes every day. Most of the time, it changes multiple times a day. Change is constant, from resident needs to family frustrations to regulatory environment challenges. Most of the time, this fact insulates us from believing we have all the answers.

When a manager creates an environment where the team feels like they have all the answers, it squashes innovation. People do not look for new solutions; they simply follow directions. Yet, there are many managers out there who believe they know everything. If you believe you're the smartest person in the room, find a new room or adopt a new perspective. Leaders seek knowledge and understanding; they are not afraid of being wrong or implementing the ideas of others. You must have a burning desire to learn as much as possible for as long as you possibly can.

I previously collaborated with a chief-level operator who was highly successful throughout most of his career. He was intelligent with a great deal of applicable experience in post-acute care. He led multiple organizations to incredible levels of success from financial and business perspectives. In short, he experienced success in all measurable areas of business. But at some point in his storied career, his approach and mindset began to shift. He was no longer interested in learning. He believed he had all the answers because he had seen so many situations and experienced so many things over the long course of his career. His vast experience led him to believe he didn't need to learn anything else. He had an established track record and an effective playbook.

And so, as times and needs changed, his playbook remained the same: a disastrous combination. His three main focus areas were reducing expenses, growing census, and leveraging vendor relationships. He did not care how cutting costs would almost certainly negatively impact care delivery or morale throughout the organization. He did not mind demanding that people take care of more residents with fewer resources. As most of us understand, census is the number one generator of revenue in our care setting: More census plus less expenses equals more profits. He was also extremely focused on leveraging vendor relationships.

These actions made the organizations he led a poor partner for the vendors, which then provided a subpar service to the staff and residents. The care setting had changed. Quality and relationships matter more than ever. The old playbook is no longer effective, and it's never been a sustainable solution. This approach of reducing expenses, increasing census, and negatively leveraging vendor relationships led to the closing of organizations, unsustainable outcomes, fractured relationships, and, in some cases, legal actions against the entities that followed this direction.

This all stemmed from refusing to learn, refusing to adjust to the changes in the markets and communities we serve, and the dangerous conviction that he had all the answers. You stop growing as a leader when you stop seeking knowledge and think that you understand everything because you've experienced a lot. It's a very dangerous place that will eventually lead to negative outcomes. This approach will undoubtedly lead to increased turnover, damaged morale, census declines, and a negative impact on all measurable business performance metrics. Learning is critical to the success of leaders.

Lead by Example

As a leader, when you listen to your people and have a strong desire to learn, you are well on your way to leading by example. There is no faster way to build rapport with your team than for you to demonstrate your willingness and ability to do everything you ask of them, rolling up your sleeves and being the positive influence that they need to become great leaders themselves. You must be capable of leading from the front, unafraid of failure, unfazed by challenges, and humble enough to let them see you stumble. Habits are contagious; choose them wisely. Your people will follow your example, good or bad.

They don't necessarily follow what you say but will absolutely recognize and follow what you do. You, as the leader, promote what you permit. The actions and behaviors that you allow throughout the home, with your staff, your residents, and your families, are the things you're promoting. When you allow negative things to occur without correction, those things are witnessed by all of your employees, the top and bottom performers. The bottom performers are going to take it as a "green light" to continue their poor performance because it is accepted by you, their leader. The top performers will leave because they won't want to be in an environment where those things are permitted. Nick Saban, legendary head football coach at the University of Alabama, described this mindset when he said, "Mediocre people hate high achievers, and high achievers hate mediocre people."

Another potential negative side-effect of permitting poor behavior is that those negative character traits will rub off on other staff members. Those team members who are new or on the fence, so to speak, will recognize that poor behavior is acceptable and will adapt accordingly. If this goes on long enough, you will be left with a team of mediocre people, and all your high achievers will be working for the competition. You must recognize and accept the fact that you are promoting the behaviors you permit in your home. If you do not appreciate the current actions and outcomes of your team, look at their leader first.

You have the duty and responsibility to lead by example. You should be the ideal employee: You should demonstrate everything you want to see, feel, and hear from your employees. If you want loyal employees who will run through a wall for you, show them first how much you are willing to do for them.

The most recent and relevant example of leading by example comes from my personal life. For a long time, I lived a mostly stagnant lifestyle. After work, I would enjoy an alcoholic beverage, sit around, and do nothing, all in the name of relaxation. Fitness wasn't a big part of my life, and I didn't pay much attention to what I consumed. I have gone through phases of my life where fitness and nutrition mattered to me, but I have been incredibly inconsistent. I have three children. At the time of writing this book, two of them are teenagers. I started to realize they paid more attention to my actions than my words. What I was doing mattered much more than what I was saying. My kids don't listen to every single thing I say, but they certainly pay attention to the things that I do: my actions, my choices, and my behaviors.

For a long time, I would tell my older two kids how important it was to work out and fuel their bodies properly. I would preach about the importance of going to practice and putting in extra work outside of practice that others are not willing to do. But I was not living those words in any way. I was not putting in any extra work. I was not fueling my body properly. I was not winning. I was showing my children—the best and most important part of me—how to lose.

As a result, it was a constant battle to get them to do any of the things I knew were necessary for them to be successful while I was sitting on the couch barking orders. My stagnant lifestyle really started to stand out to me, and I realized I needed to be the change that I wanted to see in them. Three years ago, I discovered 75 Hard, and I quietly went to work on myself. I was working out, I was fueling my body properly, I was making good decisions, and, most importantly, I wasn't drinking alcohol. My son and oldest daughter witnessed my mental and physical transformation. They recognized that I was becoming a different and better human, a better father, and a better example. The behaviors of reading every day, drinking water, and working out consistently started to spill over into their daily routines. They both started packing their own lunch, paying attention to proteins and carbohydrates. They started lifting weights outside of team workouts and started to join me during some of my outdoor cardio sessions. When my example changed, their behaviors changed. My actions influenced more than my voice ever could have.

Today, they are both focused on improving themselves and positively influencing their little sister. At times, they're reading books of their own volition. They still spend too much time on their phones, like every other teenager in the world, but they do incorporate some reading. They're in the gym before or after school. It isn't such a struggle to get them to practice and to put in a little extra work with the free time that they have. They are choosing to sharpen their skills themselves, and I talk about it less than I ever have before. It's less of a struggle because I'm showing them instead of telling them.

The same thing occurs with our employees. They will follow what you do much more closely than what you say. As their leader, being able to do what you're asking them to do is one of the most important characteristics of leadership. It's my belief that, as a leader, you should be one of the most talented people in the areas you're in charge of. When someone comes to you for help, you should be able to pull from a bucket of experience. You should be able to discuss how you dealt with a similar situation when you were in their shoes. That creates credibility, trust, and grace, all elements you need to be a great leader. Grow your leadership muscle through experience and grow your people through your willingness to share those experiences and lessons learned so their journey may be a little smoother.

As we wrap up our L-phase, understand that these three elements are critically important to the overall leadership model. You have to listen to seek understanding. You have to listen to what your team is bringing to you without judgment, without qualifying it as good or bad. Understand the good exists because they are coming to you with their challenges. If they are bringing their challenges to you, they believe that you care enough and have the ability to help. If it's ever quiet or if somebody is not bringing you their challenges, don't assume the challenges don't exist. Assume they're not bringing them to you for a reason. Consider this a big red flashing light indicating that you need to go out and solicit feedback and ask questions to discover what your team is dealing with.

As a strong leader, be open-minded. You have to understand how valuable it is to learn and care about their challenges. You need to be the resource they trust and will come to when things go wrong. You don't need to be the smartest person in the room. You need to create a room where all of the smart people are willing to visit, explore, and share ideas without fear of failure or judgment. Create an environment where people want to learn and want to bring information for you to learn. That will create an incredibly talented team that works together to find new solutions and break through barriers—together!

Don't stand on top of the mountain telling everyone how to do everything. Roll up your sleeves and help them. Inspire them through action. You want a leader who has experience in the exact area where you're facing challenges—a leader who is willing to share ideas, philosophies, concepts, and even failures to demonstrate understanding and relatability. People do not want a manager; they want a leader who will be there with them when the struggle is testing them. When things get tough, people want someone they can turn to and learn from. That's how you're going to grow your people.

Becoming a great listener who is constantly learning will help you to lead by example, and these traits will give you a solid foundation as we start our LEGACY Leadership journey. Many business concepts and management approaches encourage you to remove emotion. We *feel* differently. We believe that emotions are necessary to be a complete leader. Until Artificial Intelligence replaces us all, we will continue to incorporate emotion into our model, starting with empathy.

A LEGACY Leader...

...Leads with Empathy

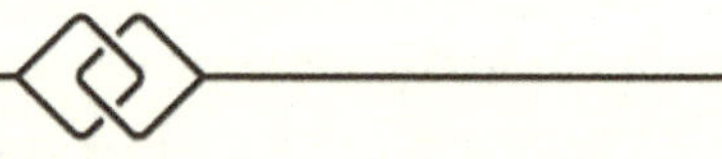

As a leader, many situations require you to simply focus on the facts and leave emotion completely out of your decision-making. However, to be an effective leader, you must possess the ability to take on another's perspective, to understand, feel, share, and possibly respond to their experience, which is empathy. With that approach, you can experience the feelings, understand the challenges of those you lead, and help navigate with empathetic support as a leader. The ability to bring emotion into leadership appropriately is a rare and valuable skill: to support your team, focus on their feelings, focus on them as individuals, and help put the individual ahead of the mission so that the individual will put the mission first.

A large national organization had recently acquired a large facility in the desert just outside of Las Vegas. As this home was going through the transition process of moving from one organization to another, the CEO of their new operations company came to visit. This was going to be the newest facility in his portfolio. This CEO was an extremely busy person, as most are. He was responsible for nearly 200 homes across the country, over 15,000 residents, and more than 45,000 employees. Yet he felt it necessary to visit the new home and personally welcome the team, residents, and families to his organization.

As he toured the home during his visit, he noticed an employee with a cigarette pack in her shirt. As someone who was an extremely healthy individual and valued his own physical and mental health as well as that of his people, he asked what it would take for her to quit smoking. She responded with a bit of small talk and laughed off the idea, indicating that she wasn't interested in quitting. She joked about it a little bit, but he was very serious: He immediately offered to pay for whatever she needed to make sure that she had the necessary resources available to her to quit smoking. He was putting himself in her shoes and experiencing all of the adverse effects of smoking right along with her. He could see that the act of smoking was hurting her, and as a highly empathetic leader, it was also hurting him.

A couple of years later, I asked the CEO why he took this approach. He told me that as a leader, he wanted to minimize the suffering of his staff. Even when they could not see the suffering, he would experience it with them and do his best to respond to alleviate as much of it as possible.

He cared about her as an individual. During his initial conversation with the employee, he turned to the Vice President of Operations in charge of that home, and he made sure the VP understood the importance of this employee being able to get whatever help she needed to stop smoking. There were no conditions attached, and nothing in it for him other than caring about the individual, wanting her to be as healthy as possible and quit the dangerous habit.

A year later, this facility experienced a ton of success (more on that later). The CEO returned to celebrate with the team because this building, when acquired a year prior, was a bottom performer that had grown to new heights. While there, he looked for a single, very specific employee. He absolutely remembered her and wanted to know if she had quit smoking and if she had gotten the support that she needed from the vice president.

Unfortunately, when he found her, she had not quit smoking. When the CEO asked what the vice president did to help her, she told him that he tried but did not go much beyond the initial offer of support. *She didn't want help.* Unfortunately, that is where the conversation ended. She didn't want to quit, and he didn't push it any further. The VP was focused on everything he thought was most important to turn around a massive home that was failing on multiple fronts. However, he was about to learn a valuable lesson in what was actually important.

No one was expecting the CEO to ask that question or to find that employee and see if she had quit smoking, especially not the vice president. But I tell you, the VP learned an extremely valuable lesson in empathy and leadership that day. He learned to care about the human connection and the importance of supporting people beyond the business metrics.

Now, while this person may or may not still be smoking today, I am fortunate enough to call that former vice president a friend.

He is now a very successful Chief Operating Officer of a medium-sized regional organization and cares deeply about his people. He consistently connects to their *why* and is willing to do whatever is necessary to support his people. That valuable lesson from this gracious CEO has had a tremendous ripple effect because he connected to that person on a human level. He tapped into the empathy element of leadership. He cared about the individual and was willing to do whatever was necessary to make her better, regardless of the business metrics or what it meant for him as a CEO. He cared about humans, and through his actions, he inspired a vice president to grow as a leader. The CEO has since passed away, but his legacy lives on through the countless leaders he grew during his time on this Earth. He made it part of his life's mission to understand, feel, and respond to the needs of others. As a result, he was an extraordinary leader who appropriately used emotion to grow his people.

The empathy shown that day had a tremendous effect that is still positively impacting the post-acute care setting today. Empathy is vital to leadership, and the most valuable part of empathy is when leaders can connect to the *why* of their people. You have to understand their perspective. You have to understand *why* they do what they do on a regular basis. *Why* do your employees choose to work in post-acute care? *Why* do they choose to work at your home? What inspires them every day? You have to understand those things so you can support those efforts, establish an emotional connection with them, and inspire them to go beyond just the basics of getting the job done and take it to the next level. You have to care enough to understand your team and help them understand the critical elements necessary to accomplish the mission.

Equally important is helping the team understand the things that aren't as critical: Items we could minimize to create more overall satisfaction and the completely unimportant things that we can eliminate in order to focus more time on the critical tasks. This all starts with understanding the *why*: what people are motivated by, what they're inspired by, *why* they choose to work in post-acute care, *why* they choose to be on your team, and what is important to them in the future.

What does their growth path look like? You have to understand what gets them out of bed every day. The most satisfying work environments are created when there's mission alignment—when you can connect your organization's mission to the goals or the individual team member's *why*. Mission alignment will lead to inspiration and ensure that your team will push through challenges and discover new ways around obstacles.

Motivation is temporary, but inspiration can last much longer. When you connect to somebody's *why*—when you can align your mission, your goals, and what you are trying to achieve with what is important to them—a beautiful thing happens: your team can and will move mountains for you.

It all starts with empathy and caring enough to seek the understanding of what's important to your employees. Understand the individuals. Each person has a different answer to the questions above. It is your responsibility as the leader of your department, home, or organization to understand the motivations of all those people so that you can connect with them on a personal level. Much like the CEO who connected with the employee who smoked, this understanding ultimately led to the growth of her supervisor, who now impacts countless other people. One simple element, one simple ask, and one effort of caring enough to go beyond the business did not seem like much at the time, but it is still producing positive results all these years later.

The book *All In* by Adrian Gostick and Chester Elton contains a great case study with a powerful discovery that, in part, highlights the importance of the emotional side of leadership. The case study covers ensuring mission alignment, much like we just discussed, and, as a result, creating engaged, empowered, and energized employees. In this case study, the large organization Towers Watson studied 700 organizations across the globe. Of these 700, there were 25 that stood out in all business performance areas. They stood out two to three times ahead of the other 675 organizations. They had better retention rates, generated more revenue, had happier employees, and had a more successful business model. Through this study, they searched for the common traits of these top performers. They wanted to identify the critical and common traits that existed in all 25 of these top-performing companies. They found that they had engaged, enabled, and energized employees (Source: *All In*, 2012 Gostick & Elton).

Leaders created high levels of engagement. Employees felt strong levels of attachment to the company, which made them willing to consistently put forth extra effort. That engagement was much like what we just discussed with connecting to your team's *why*. When these organizations and individuals had mission alignment, it created a level of engagement where people were inspired, motivated to go beyond the basics, and excited to do a little bit extra. Great leaders create engaged employees. You create engaged employees by connecting to their *why* and ensuring it aligns with your mission so that you are both satisfied when you accomplish those goals.

The second characteristic of these employees was that they were enabled. This study showed that these organizations created environments that supported productivity and autonomy, which led to employees feeling enabled. They had the tools that they needed, clear direction to understand what the mission of the organization was, and the autonomy to go out and create solutions for any and all challenges. Now, this group of employees are not only aligned with your mission, but they're also enabled. They have the freedom to solve problems in the most efficient and effective way possible. They have clear direction and understanding of the goals, and they have all the tools required to accomplish the mission. The third element of this trifecta is energy. The leaders had employees who had a great sense of well-being and drive at work. They were energized.

When you align with their mission and provide them with the tools and the autonomy, they get excited about the work. They're excited about the mission, and they care about accomplishing it. When you, as a leader, care about the physical, social, and mental well-being of your employees, that will create an energized environment that promotes innovation and inspiration—where satisfaction is inevitable and where great things are going to happen because people are aligned with your mission. They have the right tools and direction to get there and are excited to accomplish it alongside you.

While each of those elements ties into empathy and the feeling side of leadership—make no mistake about it—they lead to measurable business outcomes in the areas of revenue, turnover, staff engagement, and employee retention. Appropriately incorporating empathy into leadership will create engaged, enabled, and energized employees who will be focused on the metrics because you are focused on the people.

Let's take a look at what happens when a manager creates an environment that is lacking in empathy. We collaborated with a small 100-year-old community in a tiny town in Central Illinois. They had been a staple in the small farming community and one of the area's main employers.

Shortly after our collaboration started, the community, a religious-based nonprofit, was sold to a private investor. We did not know it then, but the new owner had been a post-acute owner for years with a very questionable track record. The new owner valued profits over everything else; he cared very little for the residents and even less for the staff. He wanted the home to grow census and reduce expenses as quickly as possible. Most of the leadership team had been with the home for years, some for decades. In the months leading up to the change of ownership, we were able to collaborate with the team directly, and we started to make progress.

The census was growing, and the team was energized. While we did not have the ability to give them additional resources, we gave them hope. They started to believe and take action to make a turnaround possible. For the first time in over two years, they experienced their first month in the black. Unfortunately, the sale was already in motion and beyond our control.

The new owner did not spend any time getting to know anyone on the team outside of the administrator. He took no interest in learning about the history of the home, the needs of the market, or the individuals that comprised the team. After meeting with him for the first time, I knew immediately that mission alignment would never occur. We would not be aligned, but this was ultimately of little concern as our relationship was temporary. I feared that there would be no mission alignment with the team that had been part of this community for so long.

The first order of business was to increase the private pay rates in the skilled nursing facility and the rent of the independent living apartments. The new owner did not consider the fixed income of the tenants; he simply saw the possibility of increasing revenue without having to add any new residents or increase costs. He also put a freeze on hiring new positions or giving any type of pay increase. Then, he ensured that all decision-making flowed through him. The team had zero autonomy. The one area where he did allow an increased budget—almost insisting on it—was in the dietary department. He believed that having food that was "delicious and nutritious" would be an extremely important competitive advantage.

Residents, families, staff, community members, and local referral sources all expressed concerns over the changes and the community's future. Various people shared stories about how valuable this home was to the community and how important it is to offer an affordable option to community members, many of whom had rarely experienced life outside of their small town. Residents and employees desired to remain local, but new ownership made that more difficult by the day. These feelings and concerns were ignored. New outside vendors were brought into the home, and local relationships were damaged. The reputation as a place to work and a place to live suffered. Staff became frustrated and started to leave. Referrals slowed, and admissions stopped.

After a number of disagreements and continued confirmations that our mission would never align with his intentions, we gave our notice that we would no longer collaborate with this home. It was a decision I struggled with for a long time because I cared about the residents and staff. I felt like I had become their only voice and advocate. We did our best to coach the team and make a smooth exit, attempting to leave the team in a better place than we found them. The hardest part is that we knew exactly where this path would lead for the home, staff, and residents.

The new owner never attempted to see, feel, or experience the challenges through the eyes of the staff, residents, or community members. He had very little concern for anyone or anything outside of the profitability of the home. The mission did not matter. There was no attempt to understand, let alone connect with the *why* of anyone. Resources were reduced. Autonomy was eliminated. Employee engagement and energy disappeared, and census and revenue went right along with it. Not surprisingly, the home did not survive.

A home that was part of a community for a century was destroyed by one owner who decided to ignore empathy.

Less than one year after the purchase, this home was sold again and converted into an adult daycare facility. A few years later, during the height of COVID, we heard an unexpected but not surprising update about the former owner. The United States Attorney's Office for the Northern District of Illinois reported, "The owner of several Illinois nursing homes has been indicted by a federal grand jury for allegedly skimming money from federally insured facilities that had defaulted on mortgage loans to pay expenses of a non-federally insured facility." Unfortunately, the greed of one caused the suffering of many.

Empathy is a vital part of your leadership toolbox. You have to be able to understand what the people that you are leading are experiencing, the challenges they are facing, the barriers to their success, and what you can do to reduce those barriers or eliminate them altogether. As author and motivational speaker Simon Sinek instructs, start with their *why*. You have to give them the tools, support, and freedom to be successful. You have to create an environment where the energy is strong and positive, where excitement is encouraged, and where you celebrate wins together so that people are inspired to make a difference and contribute. The ultimate leadership win happens when they are fulfilling their own purpose by contributing to your mission.

As you inspire your team to discover new solutions, they will stumble from time to time. Failure is a very important part of growth. Mistakes teach us valuable lessons that success never can. For your team to succeed, you have to create an environment where failure is accepted and honest mistakes are celebrated. Grace is the leadership trait that will give your team the confidence to explore new solutions and learn along the way.

A LEGACY Leader...

...Extends Grace

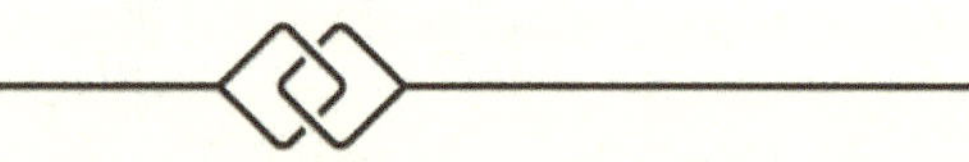

Historically, there's been an adversarial relationship between sales and clinical leadership in post-acute care. It's always been a bit contentious. Some liaisons want to put heads in beds, while clinicians want to provide excellent quality care. Sales is money-motivated. Clinical teams are motivated by quality. Obviously, these are general statements and not always 100% true, but most of the time, sales professionals are motivated by the potential of earning a bonus. Clinical leadership is usually motivated by healing people, watching them progress through their treatment plan, and being able to discharge back into the community successfully. Very few sales professionals create a strong enough relationship with their clinical teams. I've always focused on the relationship with my clinical counterpart and worked towards building a foundation of trust. Building trust helps to create an environment where grace can grow. Grace leads to forgiveness, and forgiveness is critical in post-acute care because mistakes are going to happen.

To build a strong relationship with clinical leaders, I always attempted to put myself in their shoes and understand how to review referrals through their eyes. I wanted to learn what they were comfortable and uncomfortable with from a clinical standpoint. And most importantly, I wanted to understand *why*. My goal was to understand what I would need to do to gain their trust. I wanted to know what training the staff needed, what tools, and what equipment would make them more confident in their ability to meet the clinical needs of residents they were historically uncomfortable caring for. I learned how mistakes during the assessment and/or admissions process negatively impact the building. I paid close attention to how the staff is impacted when we admit a challenging resident. It has a negative effect on the team, the resident, and the home when we admit a resident for which we do not have the proper training or the necessary equipment. I became acutely aware of all the challenges that come along with getting those things in place after the admission had already occurred. A mentality that I believe separated me from other sales professionals as I was getting started is that from very early on, I fully understood and focused on the fact that my success simply meant more work for everyone else. When I was successful, that meant we were growing the census, taking care of more humans, many times without additional resources.

That part has always been exciting for me. I looked at the census numbers like a scoreboard. It was a reflection of my hard work and a measurement of my effectiveness. As a sales professional, these efforts were rewarded with the opportunity to earn monthly bonuses. Most other positions within the post-acute care setting do not have the same opportunity. The other staff members who were given more work as a result of my success did not receive any additional compensation. I'm giving them more residents to care for, more medications to pass, more trays to pass, more family meetings to conduct, and potentially more challenges. My successes simply meant more work for everyone else, and I understood that from Day 1.

This understanding caused me to focus on building a solid relationship with the clinical leaders and their teams. I focused on expressing my gratitude and constantly reminded myself that my success was 100% dependent on their ability to properly care for our current and future residents. As I focused on relationship-building and gratitude, we built a strong foundation for our relationship that, over time, created trust. I trusted that our clinical leaders would do everything possible to ensure their team was willing and able to practice at the top of their license. I trusted that they were going to look for ways to say "yes, if" rather than "no." This "yes, if" mentality allowed me to create a fun marketing approach where I would tell all our referral sources, "We will never say no to a referral." All of our clinical readers' hearts just skipped a beat or two. We wouldn't say "no," we would say "yes, if," and the condition that the "if" represents might never happen.

For example, if they referred a bariatric patient who exceeded the weight limit for our mechanical lift, I might say something like, "Yes, if this patient can lose 250 pounds so that we can safely transfer them with our mechanical lift, we will happily accept them." This is one example of how focusing on building a strong relationship with the clinical team made my job a little easier and allowed me to be more successful.

The clinical leaders trusted that I had their interests in mind and that I was going to find them the right referrals, not just the available referrals. They trusted that I would prioritize quality over quantity. They trusted that, when I made a mistake, I would own it and help fix it. The trust created through gratitude helped both sides to better understand and implement grace. The one thing that we can guarantee about taking care of people is that mistakes are going to happen. This is something the best systems, processes, and policies will not change. Mistakes are unavoidable. In order for a team to thrive, there must be an environment of grace.

As I began to understand the value of grace, I became more forgiving and understanding of things that negatively impacted the census. I began to realize that when residents were sent back to the hospital or discharged early, it was not intentional—the clinical team was not sabotaging our success. I knew they were trying to do their best to provide the highest level of care for these individuals. Grace allowed me to open my heart and understand that when a resident passed away, that was a life that was lost, a human being that is no longer with us, not a negative impact on our census. Grace helped me change my mindset and think of everything from a human perspective. Grace made me a better person, a more effective sales professional, and a more committed post-acute leader. Empathy allowed me to view the world from their perspective and really attempt to understand how my mistakes would negatively impact the lives of our staff, our current residents, and our potential future residents.

The relationship-building efforts with our clinical leaders created grace on both sides. When I accepted a referral that was a challenge, they were understanding and forgiving. They educated me, showing me how not to make that mistake twice. I think the most important element of learning was understanding the *why* behind what we could and could not accept from a clinical standpoint. Once I understood the boundaries, I would respect them. I may challenge and push them to the edge of the boundary, but at the end of the day, I respected my clinical partners and trusted their guidance.

Grace helped us to create an environment in which both sides always assumed the best intentions, which is a powerful approach when mistakes are likely. As both sides made a valiant effort to understand the other's perspective, role, and responsibilities, grace emerged. We were much more understanding and forgiving when we attempted to see the challenges through one another's eyes.

I did things that made their jobs more difficult: I filled our buildings to 100% occupancy, I accepted some challenging residents with challenging family members, I gave last-minute notice about admissions, and I made promises about care, private rooms, or shower schedules that our team would need to deliver on. They did things that made my job a little tougher: They said no to referrals, they had customer service failures that led to people leaving our home, and they had poor survey outcomes at times. At the end of it all, grace allowed us to understand one another better, forgive each other, focus on the good, and learn from the mistakes. "Grace" was instrumental in our growth as a team and success as an organization.

One of the most important elements of grace is that it allows you to create an environment where it is safe to fail. You must create an environment where your people are not afraid to take risks because innovation will stall in such a situation. When people are worried about the possibility of making a mistake, when they operate in an environment where they are afraid to fail—innovation halts, and solutions are slow. Most of the time, this causes great leaders and great employees to be unsatisfied and unfulfilled.

As a result, they seek to discover an environment where they can spread their wings, where they can explore, where they can learn and where they can safely fail. Through grace, you will create an environment where it is safe to fail. Because if it's not, you will create an environment where fear leads to stagnation, and people will do nothing in an attempt to avoid failure. Ironically, the approach of creating an environment where perfection is the expectation always leads to failure. As a leader, it is your responsibility to help your team become excited about the possibilities and not afraid of the "what ifs."

A great example of a time when failure was frowned upon, when it did not feel safe to fail in post-acute care, was during the COVID pandemic. In March of 2020, we all felt like we could not fail. There were so many unknowns. Most leaders were very afraid to take any chances outside the state or federal recommendations. Many companies took all the recommendations very seriously and literally. Most of the recommendations, if not all, resulted from government officials and medical professionals attempting to create a safe environment for our staff, residents, and families. There were many unknowns, and therefore, these recommendations were changing on a very regular basis. Great intentions, but COVID and all these recommendations created an environment where everyone was afraid to fail. This approach squashed any and all innovation. People were afraid to take any risks because there was a lot that was unknown, and you did not want to be responsible for the death or suffering of any human.

As a result, many organizations stopped accepting admissions. At times, these holds were due to an outbreak; at other times, it was due to a staffing constraint because many staff left due to fear, and others were unable to work for 14 days at a time. It was not long before the census plummeted. Unfortunately, many of those organizations still have not fully recovered. Whether it's census or staff that left during COVID, many have not returned. However, there are some companies that created an environment where innovation was part of the solution and where they were willing to take calculated risks. I don't mean that they were willing to put the safety of residents or staff at risk. Instead, they were willing to look at the facts, look at the science, and make some decisions that were on the fringe of state and federal recommendations. It is no surprise those same organizations are back to pre-COVID census levels, with many of them fully staffed and continuing to grow.

The most significant fact is that many of these places created an environment where it was not safe to fail. They took a very conservative approach to everything, and yet they did not perform any better from a regulatory or quality standpoint than those who took some calculated risks. Their infection rates are not significantly better, and their overall performance is not stronger than that of those who have adapted to the new conditions. These leaders created an environment where it was safe to fail and embraced innovation.

From my personal experience with these forward-thinking organizations, grace was the foundation of their environment that created innovation, led to inspiration, and allowed people to take intelligent risks in order to go outside of the norm to find success. COVID had a lot of negative effects, but some people rose. Some leaders understood that they had to go outside what was being recommended, and they had to make some tough decisions, take calculated risks, and create an environment where it was safe to fail. Grace allowed for that.

When you create an environment where failure is frowned upon 100% of the time, it will lead to failure. You have to incentivize innovation. You have to create an environment where it's exciting to discover new solutions. When compared to other healthcare settings, most of the time, post-acute care is very slow to change and very slow to innovate. For example, we are slow to bring technology or new solutions to our care setting. Grace will allow you to create an environment where people become comfortable taking chances. Again, taking calculated, well-thought-out risks. We don't want to put residents or staff at risk. We don't want to jeopardize anyone's safety, but you can create an environment where people seek new solutions in an old care setting, which will help you create distance from the competition.

Grace has the ability to destroy silos. The mentality of "it's not my responsibility" will transform into a team of people who are willing to do what is required. The mentality of doing what is required is powerful and necessary for success. When your team is not worried about whose responsibility something is or who will get the credit, when they are simply focused on doing what is required for your home to be successful, you are on the right path.

Again, with grace being the foundation, when people know that it's okay to take a chance and they will be forgiven if something doesn't go perfectly, they are willing to help one another out. People desire and are willing to be part of the team if they understand the other team members value their opinions and time and genuinely care about their success. Grace helps people to understand the fact that high tides lift all boats. When we care about one another's success, we all win more often.

One of the areas where I experienced this firsthand was in a facility that had created an environment where it did not feel safe to fail regarding wound care. They had a dedicated wound care nurse who was supplied to them by a vendor, exclusively focused on wounds. This was an awesome concept. The vendor would supply a wound nurse and pass the cost on to the home. The home would receive a dedicated wound care expert who would not be pulled into any other area of responsibility. This nurse would focus on wound care and be part of the team to that extent, but nothing beyond that. It was a great idea, and it did work for a while, but eventually, it created a division between the facility staff and the wound care team.

This model created a silo and division among caregivers. There was no grace. The facility-based nurses did not desire to learn wound care and typically did not have a clear understanding of the wound care needs of their own residents. They were completely siloed and only focused on their part of the patient, which is an extremely dangerous approach to care. When you have a caregiver with tunnel vision who is not focused on the resident as a whole, you are heading for disaster. With a dedicated wound nurse, the wound skills of the other nurses declined, as did their knowledge and understanding of wound care.

As a result, the nurses did not have a comprehensive understanding of policies, treatments, or care plans related to wound care. They were not knowledgeable about the specific needs related to wounds for their residents. Not surprisingly, as a result of this approach, this home ended up getting into some significant regulatory trouble around wounds that the state attributed to the process and the program that they had installed. In this example, there was only one person in the entire home who was knowledgeable of the wound process: the outsourced nurse, who wasn't viewed as part of the team. It created division. There was no grace. There was no forgiveness. There was no element of anyone working together and creating innovative solutions. There was blame, inefficiencies, ineffectiveness, and contention. The lack of grace ultimately led to residents suffering and the home receiving financial punishment.

In order to create an environment of grace, we had to change the model. We had to put the responsibility of care back on the nurses who were part of the team in that home. The wound care nurse became a support to these nurses instead of the dedicated resource that simply took on all the care. That nurse became a resource to help these nurses learn all aspects of wound care. We focused on creating grace throughout the process. We shared with the team that, hey, they were going to stumble, they were going to make mistakes, they weren't going to be as efficient, they weren't going to be as knowledgeable at the beginning, and that all of that was absolutely acceptable and understandable.

Through grace and forgiveness, an entire facility of nurses is now much stronger when it comes to wound care. Their entire approach to quality care delivery has evolved and is no longer completely dependent on one human. They now have a team of nurses with knowledge about wounds who are motivated to learn more and provide better care. Each of these nurses now has a better understanding of their residents as a whole and is more confident to accept new residents with wound care needs.

Grace allowed for this. It created this mentality of empowerment. The people closest to the resident, the people closest to the customer, to the client, to the patients should have the authority and autonomy to capitalize on the knowledge they have. Amazing things happen when a leader is able to create an environment of autonomy and empowerment where team members do not care who receives credit for the success of the team.

Former U.S. Secretary of State Colin Powell covered this mindset as part of his leadership principles. He said, "There's no end to the good you can do if you do not care who gets credit." I think that sums it up very well. It doesn't matter who gets credit, and when we can foster an environment of grace that leads to forgiveness, there will be plenty of credit to go around. Grace is the element that creates the environment that will cause people to be inspired and innovative. It will allow them to understand that if they do misstep, it won't mean something negative for them. They're going to learn from it. As a leader, you are required to have forgiveness for the people in your command when they make mistakes.

They must clearly understand that they will be forgiven as long as their intentions were good and they stayed within moral and ethical boundaries. Earlier, we discussed the importance of being fully committed to your goals while allowing flexibility in the ways you and your team accomplish those goals. Forgiveness fosters this flexibility; it enables your team to explore ways to successfully accomplish the mission, allowing you all to achieve your goals together. Forgiveness is a leadership trait that inspires action. Your team must understand that it is acceptable to seek new solutions, and that failure or challenges will not alter the mission or the desired outcome. We are still committed to making it to New York by the fifteenth.

As leaders and members of a team, we learn from those failures. They are necessary for our ultimate success. Without failure, success is not possible; it is part of the process. Failure must be viewed as feedback; it is not final. We have to use experiences to build on and learn from our failures. Wildly successful people have failed more times than most of us have tried anything. So, you have to understand, embrace, and promote the idea that failure is not final. You have the responsibility to create an environment where grace is the foundation so that productive failure can occur, which will allow your team to learn and develop new skills along the way. Productive failure is a term we use to highlight the importance and value of failing forward. We all understand that failure is an inevitable part of the process, so why not use the failures to our advantage? Productive failure occurs when we learn a lesson and can apply a new skill set to an old situation to discover a more effective solution.

Leaders must reward the behavior that they want to encourage. Do not only reward outcomes. Don't just celebrate at the end when you achieve the final goal—celebrate the effort along the way. That's going to lead to the team discovering new solutions. You have to reward the behavior that you want to encourage. So, if you want to encourage behavior that is going to lead to innovation, then you have to be okay with failure and you have to reward effort over simply celebrating or criticizing the outcomes. Mindset coach and leader Ben Newman talks about the concept of "aggressive patience." By this, he means the idea that we must be patient and respect that the improvement process takes time, and we simultaneously need to work aggressively to make the necessary changes in our lives or within our team. Leadership is not a passive responsibility; it requires constant action and continued participation.

When you are able to embrace the emotional side of leadership and build trust, grace, and forgiveness among the team, you will create the amazing byproduct of autonomy. The best employees desire to be led but also desire to have the freedom to explore new opportunities and attempt new solutions. Your responsibility is to create the boundaries for operation. The team should clearly understand what is and is not acceptable from a moral, ethical, and legal standpoint. Grace inspires forgiveness, which leads to people feeling safe and inspired to try new things. As long as they stay within your defined operational boundaries, the possibilities are endless, and people will thrive!

Autonomy is extremely satisfying and will create more freedom for you as a leader. As your team learns new skills and develops the ability to think and execute strategic decisions, they will bring you solutions rather than problems. When they do bring you problems, it will only occur after they have attempted to solve them and realize they need your expertise. Autonomy creates future leaders rather than mindless followers. Give your team the autonomy to do what is required, and you will be amazed at how quickly they destroy silos and discover solutions—together.

Your team will receive information from families, residents, surveyors, other employees, and competitors. When they feel as though they have to go through a process of approval, of asking for permission, of coming to you with it before just solving the problem, it's going to create inefficiencies. It's going to create frustration from the employee and the resident standpoint.

Unfortunately, the experience will not be as seamless or as successful as it could be if you allowed grace to shape your environment. When the opposite occurs, your team will take that information and immediately try to turn it into action. Then, as leaders, we are able to measure the outcome free of judgment. When the outcome is less than ideal, we fix it, and we adjust. That is the responsibility of the leader.

We are trying to create a problem-solving feedback system comprised of the following steps:

- **Problem identification:** The team receives new information.
- **Proactive Solution:** They make a decision and put action behind it.
- **Positive feedback:** We offer feedback and help the team to adjust.
- **Productive outcome:** We support the team and measure the outcome.

Everyone learns throughout the process, and we start back at the beginning with the next opportunity. Crucially, however, the feedback that comprises the third step is never uncovered if there isn't grace to allow people to take those chances. We must create an environment where forgiveness is not only possible but probable.

But forgiveness and grace do have their limits. As a leader, you must also be prepared to hold yourself and your team accountable. Remember while we are flexible with our methods and forgiving of well intended efforts, we are inflexible with our standards. We will accomplish the mission and in order to do so leaders must have a strong accountability muscle. Compassionate accountability will keep you from becoming a dictator. Let's explore how we can make accountability more comfortable and effective for everyone.

SCAN THE QR CODE to dive deeper into the pillars of problem-solving, *Pillar Talk with Chris Ross*: Ep. 32 - "Problem Solving" (Spotify)

A LEGACY Leader...

...Practices Compassionate Accountability

Holding your team accountable can be one of the most challenging aspects of leadership. There is a delicate balance between accountability and another "A" word often used at the water cooler to describe a manager. For a number of reasons, accountability has gotten a bad reputation. Leaders often find it to be a challenging thing to implement. Getting comfortable with accountability is an element that is absolutely necessary for effective leadership. Accountability enhanced the experience I had with the home that I referenced during our Empathy chapter. It was a large facility in the desert of Nevada. I was fortunate to be a small part of an organization that acquired this facility and the team that was responsible for integrating them into our company. When we acquired this 260-bed home, it had a census of 180. The team was disengaged.

During the exhausting sale and acquisition process, they did not feel supported or valued by their former operations company. The organization selling this home had written them off and was in maintenance mode, counting down the days until the sale was finalized. There was very little direction being provided by the managers, there were no clear expectations of the team, and many times, they did not have the necessary resources to operate a quality home.

As a result, accountability had disappeared from the environment. No one was being held accountable. No standard had been created, and there were no individual expectations or expectations for the team as a whole. During this time, the team members began to function as individuals, singularly focused on their own survival. This was certainly a far cry from an environment where empathy and grace lead to collaboration, forgiveness, and ultimately, success.

Leadership was very weak. The mission was unclear. There was no leader in place who was focused on listening, learning, or leading by example. The goals of the home and organization were unclear, which led to uncertainty and uneasiness among the staff. They weren't sure where they were going to end up. When direction is unclear and the management team is disengaged, rumors start to flow throughout the home. People are great storytellers who seem to always have an answer for things they know very little about. Most of them are very far from true, but the lack of accountability fuels this wildfire and it spreads, quickly destroying everything in its path. Standards and accountability were foreign concepts to this team. They had been left on their own for such a long period of time that they felt lost and unsupported, and they had all but forgotten the recipe for success. As we began to support this home, we recognized that a major ingredient that was missing was accountability. We understood very quickly that we could not implement any changes and expect sustainability without accountable leaders with the skills to create a culture of accountability.

In order to foster accountability and avoid damaging the relationship with the staff by starting off on the wrong foot, we had to do it in a way that allowed the team to feel supported and not micromanaged. We had to start by creating clear, well-defined expectations and sharing the *why* behind those expectations. We shared the vision and the importance of growth with everyone at this home: the leaders, the employees, the residents, the families, and the state. We needed to clearly define the expectations, *why* we had these expectations, and what was going to occur as we accomplished each of them. We had to open the lines of communication with the entire team, including the families and residents who called this place home. They had ideas and a great deal of feedback, but they had kept quiet for so long because they did not have anyone interested in hearing them. As discussed earlier, a critical part of building trust with your team is what you, as a leader, do with the information provided to you. As the team began to share ideas and requests with us, we had the responsibility to provide them with the tools to be successful.

During the selling process, most exiting companies are not focused on the upkeep and maintenance of a home. They do the minimum necessary to keep it operational, and this was the case here. We needed to make multiple changes and upgrades to the home, none more significant than those that were identified in the ventilator unit. This unit was extremely challenging for the staff to manage. The residents were complex, their needs were constant, the equipment was complicated, and the quality of care provided was substandard. The team lacked the training, equipment, and support necessary to properly care for these residents. The previous operations company felt strongly that they did not want to close that unit. They believed it was the home's only competitive advantage and that closure would be a death sentence. The staff felt differently: They believed the majority of their financial and regulatory challenges were coming from this unit. They believed that, in order to change their reputation and trajectory, they needed to do something extreme, like close a nearly full vent unit and safely discharge all the residents.

After assessing the market and looking at the facts, we decided to listen to the staff and made the decision to close that unit. There were a lot of people who felt this was a bad decision, including senior leaders in our own organization. But as great leaders do, they trusted us and allowed us to execute. Now, we had a struggling home that was closing the one unit they were known for, and their census was about to take another dip as we had to find new homes for over 30 residents who lived in the unit. But this decision helped us build trust among the team. They felt heard, and we were giving them the support they needed.

They also needed more resources. This was a large facility that we wanted to help them grow. We wanted to show them they were able to take care of over 250 residents. One part of enabling them to do that was providing more resources in the admissions department. They needed competent people to process referrals and be able to make educated decisions on whether or not to accept them as admissions. We helped them hire and train a solid admissions team, transforming it from an inefficient one-man show to a well-oiled admissions machine that was able to process 25 referrals a day.

At this point, we were building trust by providing clear directions while giving them the tools and support necessary to make them successful. Direction and tools are major parts of accountability, but it only works when the team understands exactly what success looks like. Leaders have the responsibility to model the behavior they desire so the team can feel, envision, and experience winning.

As a leadership team, we modeled the behaviors we wanted them to experience. Our clinical leaders showed the team exactly how to care for residents, and how to improve their systems for care delivery and focus on quality. Our operations leaders built models and showed the team how to execute on things like controlling staffing costs and increasing revenue through census growth. The sales leaders showed the team how to tell an exciting story about the decision to close the vent unit and the new direction of the home. All three disciplines worked together to show the team how they could grow by over 100 residents while improving quality. We embraced the idea that we would not ask anything of the team that we were unable to do ourselves. This approach created extensive credibility. We became a valuable resource rather than a management team.

We gently molded the team. We showed them how to grow. We showed them how to lead. We showed them how to provide high-quality care and how to do everything required of them. We would sit there side by side and help them. We would show them success at every level. We led by example. All of these elements were contributing to bringing accountability back into the home.

Once we felt they understood the expectations, possessed the tools necessary to meet them, and had experienced exactly what success would look and feel like, we gave them the autonomy to execute. We showed them everything. We gave them the tools and clear direction, but then we backed off to allow them the autonomy to take the lead, knowing that we were there for support if needed. That was an important element. It allowed the team to find their own style and build the confidence necessary to sustain success. This approach made it very simple for the leadership team to set expectations because we had created credibility and trust. It would have been a completely different story had we come into this new facility and just said, "Hey, you're sitting at 180; we need you to be at 200. Get it done. We'll see you in 30 days."

Unfortunately, that's what a lot of people do, and that easily could have been the approach, but that would not have made us successful, and it would not have created any accountability. Our approach created an environment where accountability was very comfortable to practice. Expectations were clear, resources were abundant, ideal behaviors were modeled, autonomy was embraced, and support was present. These conditions made holding team members accountable simple—again, not easy, but very simple to execute.

As a result, we were confident that those expectations would be met. Fast forward one year, the building was 100% occupied. They were taking care of 260 residents, having grown by 110 from the low point after closing the vent unit. They became the most profitable home in the entire portfolio, generating more revenue than entire regions. Many things needed to happen in order for this dramatic turnaround to be possible, but the element that was at the center of this incredible transformation was accountability.

We were able to create accountability by setting clear expectations, giving them the tools and support they needed, and showing them how to properly use the tools. We also focused on showing them how to leverage our support in order to meet the expectations, and then, most importantly, we backed off to create an environment of autonomy that allowed the team to become problem-solvers. This approach allowed the support team to avoid feeling like dictators. We weren't simply holding people accountable to some unrealistic expectation. We provided them with a vision and a clear understanding of why accomplishing the mission was necessary, and then we showed them exactly how it was possible. The team was responsible for everything after that. Their belief, dedication, and hard work allowed them to achieve their highest potential. Had we approached this opportunity differently, there's no way we would have experienced the level of success and sustainability we did.

When managers decide it is easier to approach things like a dictator, they create insubordination, not inspiration. Managers who focus on telling teams what to do without providing direction, resources, and modeling end up creating animosity among the team. They may experience some success, but it is not sustainable, and they become frustrated with the team. In reality, they should be frustrated with themselves. When there's no real understanding of the needs of those that you lead, you will not be able to lead them toward growth. It will, however, certainly lead to frustration and erode credibility. Accountable leaders define the mission, why it is important that we accomplish it, how we are going to get there, and the rewards we will experience when we achieve our goals. Each of these elements is vitally important to accountability.

The team in the above story experienced extensive success. The fundamental element of their success was creating an environment that supported compassionate accountability. We cared enough to properly hold people accountable, which led to the team growing skills and confidence, and accomplishing goals they never believed possible.

At Legacy, we believe in and fully embrace compassionate accountability. Healthcare leaders are some of the most selfless people in the professional world. They are servant leaders who genuinely care about people and do not typically enjoy conflict. Due to their big hearts, selfless approach, and desire to make others happy, accountability can be very uncomfortable for them. Leaders must start with a genuine care for the individual in their trust and that team member's personal and professional success. It cannot be all about business metrics. If it's all about the "Benjamins" (cash, money, profits), leadership is beyond you. It's more important to focus on the individual and their success. When they feel they are able to fulfill their purpose, the business metrics will follow. Focus on satisfying their purpose, and they will go beyond the minimum expectation in order to meet the business needs. You must value people over profits. When you genuinely care about your people, they will care about the things that make you profitable. So again, everything starts with people. Accountability is no different.

As I highlighted throughout the story above, we have found that when the following conditions are met, accountability becomes simpler. It is never easy, but it becomes a little bit simpler when you meet these conditions:

- **You must clearly define success for the individual**. Each person on the team has to understand what the expectations are, what their role and responsibilities are, and how to be successful. How do you, as the leader, define success for that individual?

- **You must provide them with the resources necessary to be successful.** You must hear and understand their needs, help them identify what they need to be successful and help them remove any barriers that are preventing them from being successful. Help your team define their needs, identify new ways to get the tools required, and teach them to use them in their most effective manner.

- **You must show them exactly what success looks like.** As the leader you must model the behavior you want displayed. This will not only show the team that it is possible, you will also be showing them that you are capable, which will build credibility. A valuable byproduct of modeling success is that when you're not available they can reference your example so they can become independent and flourish.

And when you complete those steps:

- **You must give the team the autonomy to apply their skills**. Create boundaries but allow them to explore and grow. This approach will help your team to experience that sense of purpose and fulfillment.

When you meet these conditions, holding people accountable becomes much more comfortable. We will discuss some tactical items that may help you hold your people accountable in a way that is productive to the team rather than destructive. First, you must meet the conditions we just discussed: clear and realistic expectations, sufficient resources, adequate examples of how to meet the expectations, support, and autonomy.

When setting expectations or making corrections, you must have one-on-one conversations to ensure clarity and understanding among team members so that everybody is on the same page. You have to offer productive feedback when things aren't going down the ideal path. Leaders have to provide clear, constructive feedback, allowing their people to reflect on the areas where they are not meeting the expectations and potential solutions to this.

In order to support accountability, you must clearly define the consequences of expectations not being met. This is an area where people typically struggle because consequences have a very negative connotation. But if you meet the conditions we discussed, then the consequences become easier to enforce. Having clearly defined consequences for expectations not being met, you must enforce those consequences equally across the board regardless of position or relationship with the individual.

You have the opportunity to create credibility with your team by remaining true to your word and being consistent with enforcing the standard. Accountability is setting expectations and enforcing consequences when those expectations are not met. As long as you've met the conditions, holding your team accountable should not make you uncomfortable. It is your responsibility as a leader. Like everything else, this must start at the top. Hold the leadership team accountable, including yourself. Nobody is immune to accountability.

Start at the top by promoting what you permit. By actively promoting what you authorize, the things you accept will grow. You cannot tolerate a bad employee for any reason. Many times, we may be short-staffed or have open positions, which makes us afraid to correct negative behavior because of fear of worsening a staffing challenge. When you accept poor behavior from an employee, two negative things are going to happen.

First, other employees will likely emulate that behavior, and now you have multiple people that are doing the wrong thing.

Second, good employees will not tolerate a negative environment, and they will leave. They will get frustrated and eventually find a place where they can grow. So you will lose your quality employees, your future leaders, your biggest contributors, and you will start to create an environment where the only people sticking around are the ones with counterproductive behaviors. You have to be aware that you are promoting any behaviors that you allow. So, while you may not be encouraging it through words, you are encouraging it through actions, which is much more dangerous.

You must be direct with challenging employees. If you're vague or you only address concerns in a group setting, there are two dangerous side effects.

The challenging employees will typically assume you're not talking about them, and they will tune you out. In contrast, the great employees—the ones with the most potential—will take those concerns personally. They are usually the hardest on themselves, and this will eventually lead to burnout. Group correction causes your best people to constantly feel like they are doing something wrong and end up internalizing and personalizing the corrections, which leads to frustration. Ultimately, they're going to fall short of reaching their potential.

As a leader, you must directly and clearly communicate when you identify someone doing the right thing. This is a big part of accountability that is often missed. Celebrating victories with your staff will have so many positive effects down the road. You have to celebrate wins in order to give yourself the credibility necessary to make corrections when the time comes. You must identify when your people are doing the right thing and highlight those actions in order to inspire people to continue to go above and beyond. Recognition allows accountability to feel constructive rather than critical.

So when you recognize good behaviors and then, at a later date, identify that you need to correct a negative behavior, you will have credibility with the individual because your actions clearly show that you care about them. They understand that you are willing to celebrate successes and not simply focus on their shortcomings. People are never inspired by managers who are only good at identifying opportunities or challenges. That approach creates a negative environment where all we do is discuss negativity, which always produces more negativity.

Imagine your team as a bank account. You must deposit into them before you're able to make withdrawals. Deposits must be made on a regular basis. If you want to be able to make requests or have a productive and critical conversation, you must first deposit into your team before you can effectively withdraw or have any type of critical conversation.

At Legacy, our **GROW (Gather, Recognition, Often, Winning)** program focuses on employee recognition. Often, when we're working with clients or even at Legacy among our own team, we love to focus on acknowledging all the amazing things our people and clients do. Our GROW program allows us to do that effectively.

Gather: We bring team members together to celebrate the individual(s). Group recognition is important, and people enjoy celebrating with their peers.

Recognition: We identify specifically what's going on, what's being done well, and what we want to celebrate. It's important to be very specific with the individual and what you're recognizing. When this is done in a group setting, a beautiful byproduct is that you are telling everyone else what they need to do in order to stand out and be recognized themselves.

Often: Emphasizes that it is important to celebrate frequently. Life is stressful; we all need more fun. Celebrate more! We make sure celebrating victories is part of our culture and part of our fabric as an organization. Regardless of how small of a victory, we find something to celebrate on a very regular basis, making sure that these conversations are happening often because we believe you get more of what you focus on. So, we choose to focus on the positive.

Winning: This is for winning stories. We make sure the story is specific to the individual, and we use detailed accounts of the job done well. A vital element of the winning stories is that we must connect the stories to the purpose of the individual and the overall mission of the organization. When you can tie an individual's purpose to the organization's mission, this will resonate not only with that individual but also with the other employees who want to be recognized. Now, they will have a very clear idea of what it will take to be recognized and be a celebrated part of the GROW program. At Legacy, we often start and end our meetings, emails, and messages with our favorite phrase, "Let's GROW!"

An important mindset for leadership is the ability to focus on the difference between "one day" and "Day 1." Many times, we tell ourselves lies and stories. We talk about how we're going to change "one day." *One day*, we're going to grow as a leader. *One day*, we are going to focus on our team. *One day*, when things slow down, we'll have a chance to get organized and build a plan. *One day*, we'll do this, and *one day*, we'll do that. We consistently tell ourselves the story about *one day*. Yet *one day* never comes until you change the order of those words and say, "Day 1." You must make time to focus on accountability. Like all aspects of leadership, when it's done correctly, it's very difficult. And the conditions are never going to be perfectly ideal. You have to stop telling yourself the lie that *one day* you're going to change your approach. In order for anything to change, you have to make *one day* today.

Another mindset framework we focus on is the idea of "victim" versus "victor." When your employees feel like victims of micromanaging and work in a negative environment, they become frustrated and less productive. The *victim* mentality is dangerous among staff. It leads to helplessness, counterproductivity, and complaining, all of which negatively impact productivity, efficiency, and profitability. When we, as leaders, can create an environment where compassion and accountability thrive, our employees move from victim to victor. That's why we identify and celebrate wins daily. We give and receive constructive criticism, and we adjust and grow together.

That way, we intentionally create *victors.* They feel empowered, they desire accountability, and we both create behaviors that lead to successful, sustainable outcomes.

There are many benefits to creating a team that's built around accountability and comfortable with difficult conversations. When you create and embrace compassionate accountability, it will lead to improved team dynamics. Working together, supporting each other, celebrating wins, and creating genuine care for one another are all benefits of an accountable team. When you're able to clearly connect to the *why* of each team member, you will inspire purpose that will connect to a deeper emotional aspect of their *why* and allow team members to experience true satisfaction. When you're connected to their *why*, when you are aligned with their purpose, and when there is mission alignment, then accountability becomes part of the toolbox that we use to achieve purpose and fulfillment. It's not looked at as a negative experience. It's not looked at as micromanaging or dictatorship. It's seen as a way to help the individual grow and achieve their individual purpose and fulfillment and contribute to the mission of the organization, all of which are extremely satisfying for leaders and their teams alike.

Ultimately, accountability leads to improved performance. Happier, more fulfilled employees produce better business performance metrics, and their results become sustainable as long as the environment of accountability remains intact. We're often looking for ways to get an edge on the competition, to grow our revenue, increase our census, reduce our agency usage, or improve our quality metrics. Each one of those things can be improved through accountability. Compassionate accountability will remain in place and will lead to improved business metrics as long as you follow this approach: Put the individual at the center of the equation, focus on them, give them the tools they need to be successful, help them clearly define success, show them a great example of how to achieve success, celebrate wins, and support them throughout their journey.

Effectively driving accountability is highly dependent on your ability to communicate your mission, vision, and values to your team. Communication is a foundational element of leadership. Without it, none of this would be possible, so let's talk about it!

A LEGACY Leader...

...Utilizes Communication as the Foundation for Growth

Communication is the foundation of leadership. It's no surprise to anyone that communication is critically important to our success as leaders. Indeed, it's critically important to our success as human beings. I've experienced many environments where communication has flourished and been a focal point. I've also experienced some environments where communication was not a priority. This difference always has a profound effect on the stability and continuity of the team. When teams are rooted in strong communication, anything is possible. When it is absent, failure is likely.

During my time with a large national post-acute provider, I was fortunate enough to be part of an elite team of business executives, the SWOT Team. Our team focused on exploring strengths, weaknesses, opportunities, and threats of the homes in our portfolio—not the badass Special Weapons and Tactics (SWAT) team that the regular police call when things get a little intense (if that's what you were thinking). This was one of my favorite professional experiences. We were a small team of individuals who reported directly to the Chief Marketing Officer, and we had the ability to support homes anywhere across the country, which provided many unique opportunities across the portfolio.

We were handpicked based on our skill set. A huge part of the selection process was based on our ability to communicate effectively. As bottom-performing homes were identified in the organization, a SWOT Team member would be assigned to them for eight weeks. Our responsibility during those eight weeks was to identify the areas of opportunity, address those opportunities with the local leadership team, help guide them to identify solutions to capitalize on these opportunities, and assist them to formulate sustainable plans. Not only did our solutions need to improve their performance quickly, but we also had to ensure the improvements would be sustainable long after our exit at the end of our eight-week assignment.

This environment forced us to be extremely effective communicators. We were assigned to homes in any market across the country, which usually meant we had little to no market intelligence and very few, if any, local relationships to leverage. We needed to be very confident in our ability to assess the situation, communicate the opportunities, and help the team identify solutions to those opportunities through effective communication. Our leader, who was strong but quiet, valued communication over almost every other skill. He did an amazing job of listening. We knew his door was always open, his phone was always on, and that we could bring him our biggest challenges with our potential solutions. He was great at helping us see the potential flaws in our solutions. He was also very gifted at removing barriers that we needed removed in order to achieve success. He valued communication with the team, which caused the entire team to value it as well. We always leaned on one another. We never hesitated to pick up the phone and ask for help from our teammates or simply share ideas of what was working and what was not. The group was small, and we were spread all across the United States, but we constantly communicated with each other to figure out best practices and to learn from one another the things we didn't know as individuals. When we were in the same area or the same market, we would hang out outside of work and problem-solve.

We competed with each other, but we absolutely cheered for one another and celebrated everyone's success. We always had one another's back. We certainly wanted to make sure that the SWOT Team remained elite through our outcomes and our ability to communicate wins. We were the most effective team in the organization, and many of us still have strong relationships and communicate on a regular basis today, more than ten years later.

I experienced the complete opposite with an organization we collaborated with in Colorado. They had a very weak and ineffective manager who was placed in a senior position based on a relationship, not on a skill set. The senior manager promoted an ineffective mid-level manager. That mid-level manager thought they knew best and had no reason to discuss their plans with the team. As managers do, this individual negatively influenced the team, and the people below them stopped valuing communication. This manager didn't want to hear about problems or challenges, mainly because they didn't have any experience in solving the challenges, and that would effectively expose them as an ineffective leader.

In order to avoid that situation, this individual would rather hear nothing at all. They also allowed their ego to get in the way of communication and hated to be challenged, which made growth nearly impossible. This created an environment where people did not communicate with one another. Problems grew, and they were rarely solved. They just continued to compound over time. The plans were never collaborative or sustainable. The few times that any success was achieved or experienced, it was merely luck. The lack of communication prevented collaboration and team building. The team functioned as individuals and could not duplicate or sustain even the smallest level of success.

Unfortunately, this company did not survive two full years in the state of Colorado. This failure was a result of poor leadership and terrible communication, which led to a very predictable outcome. Most of the time, when communication is not the foundation on which the team is built, the team cannot flourish, and this was true for this organization.

As we keep those stories in mind, let's discuss how to communicate effectively. You must start by creating an environment where people feel comfortable bringing their challenges to you. The team should understand that the most effective way to enlist your help is to identify a challenge, attempt a solution, and, when unsuccessful, ask you to help guide them toward a more successful solution. When your team comes to you, it starts with your listening skills. Remember, we discussed listening during the L-phase. We must hear them.

In order to illustrate the importance of hearing people at Legacy, we formulated **HEAR**, which stands for **Helping Everyone Achieve Results**. Leaders must HEAR with the goal of understanding. We don't need to focus on problem-solving while our team brings us their challenges. We can do that together after we effectively understand their concerns.

A great communicator will ask open-ended, thoughtful questions. If someone can effectively answer your question with a single word, a "yes" or a "no," it's not a great question. Get great at asking open-ended, thoughtful questions that will inspire conversation. A great self-test you can do at any point during a conversation is to measure who is doing most of the speaking. If it is you, make an adjustment. Remember, effective communication starts with listening. If you're doing the majority of the talking, then you're not listening. Make sure your side of the conversation is focused on fact-finding around their current challenges and attempted solutions. Provide confirming feedback to ensure you understand the information being provided.

Active listening requires you to rephrase key items in your own words. This approach to the conversation will ensure you have a solid understanding of the information, and it will show your team members that you are actively listening to their needs or concerns. When you HEAR their needs and concerns, and you are able to summarize them in your own words, this verifies and validates that you are truly listening and that you care about what the team has to say.

Be mindful of your tone of voice and your body language. You want to be welcoming and supportive. A warm presence that's free of judgment will go a long way to create a productive, effective conversation. Try to have conversations in areas that are free of distractions. We want to avoid being distracted by our phones, outside noises, other employees, or a stack of paperwork on our desk that we know we have to get to. To improve communication, be present, completely in the moment, and focused on the individual. When communicating, avoid multitasking. Be focused on the individual. Don't let your phone, your smartwatch, or any other piece of technology be a distraction. Do not try to rush the conversation. Make sure you have adequate time set aside so that you can focus on the individual and make them feel heard and hopefully understood. Try not to have these conversations in any kind of public area. We want people to be able to express themselves freely, so try to set aside time and space to have a private, productive conversation. Do not damage the trust with this individual or group of individuals by sharing any information that was provided.

During these conversations, focus on the facts. Don't get caught up in opinions or gossip. Communication is an area where feelings have the potential to cause more harm than good. While there are elements of leadership that should involve our feelings (such as empathy and grace, discussed previously), communication should be focused and rooted in facts and not feelings. Find the facts and focus on those areas while providing feedback.

As a leader, it is your responsibility to put action behind the items that your team brings to you. That action can take many forms, but when a team member brings you their concerns or challenges, it's important to act on the information provided or to explain why you do not feel action is necessary. You owe it to your team members to do something with the information. They are expressing their trust and belief in you as a leader by bringing you this information. Do not take that lightly.

Many times, these conversations are uncomfortable for the employee. They are already frustrated or feeling defeated by the time they get to you. Nothing will destroy trust faster than a leader who takes information and doesn't do anything with it. Employees will only bring you their challenges if they believe you are willing and capable of helping them. You must be willing and able to support your team through action as they bring you opportunities or challenges. If they stop giving you feedback, they have either lost faith in your ability to help them, or they have stopped believing that you care enough to help.

Either condition represents a failure of leadership. Therefore, it is incredibly important to focus on "action" related to the communication from your team members. If there is no action to be taken, explain why this is the case so they understand you are not dismissing them. You don't want to do anything to erode that trust and prevent future communication. There are numerous benefits to an environment that's built on effective communication. Trust is created through effective communication and reinforced with your follow-through. As we just discussed, people begin to trust in a leader that they believe understands them and cares enough to help them be successful.

When you place your team members' personal and professional goals at the forefront of your focus, you will build trust with that team, and they will be willing to follow you anywhere. Trust will grow when you follow through on what you say you're going to do. Be a person of your word, and trust will follow. Trust will continue to prosper in an environment where leaders openly share solutions and are always willing to place the team's needs ahead of their own.

One of the most frustrating things a leader can do is to try to safeguard the answers or keep information from the team. You should create an environment where you are openly sharing solutions and best practices, and you're not intimidated by the growth of your team members as leaders themselves. In some cases, they will even outgrow you. That simply means you're doing leadership right, and you should be proud. Don't be afraid of it; embrace it.

Communication will be destroyed if there's negative talk from the top. If the only thing the team hears is criticism, conversations will slow, and growth will cease. Communication will also be negatively impacted if a manager doesn't act on the information provided or does not follow through on the commitments that they have made.

You must ensure that everybody clearly understands their roles and responsibilities, which leads to team members being able to experience fulfillment. Communication grows productive, efficient, and effective employees. The better you can communicate, the more clearly you can define goals and expectations, and the more productive, efficient, and effective your employees will be.

Communication also improves the relationship between team members, leaders, and the organization as a whole. It allows for faster conflict resolution. A team that can communicate can problem-solve together. It's the foundation of creating a positive work environment where team members want to support each other and accomplish the mission. It creates an environment where employees feel empowered to act on opportunities and provide information to leadership because they believe the leaders will act on that information. Communication creates positive interactions between employees, residents, families, and other leaders. You embrace communication to create positive interactions at every level of the organization, including with customers, residents, and families.

Keep in mind that communication is a marathon, not a sprint. Leaders must clearly understand that consistency is key when you're working to improve communication. You must work on the skills that contribute to communication daily. You have to actively seek conversations. You have to solicit feedback from your team, especially if you are new to the team or your leadership role. You have to be out on the floor with those individuals, understanding their challenges and asking them for feedback. They aren't going to simply bring you things if you sit in your office behind a closed door and don't understand their environment, their challenges, their opportunities.

In order to start creating an environment where communication is valued, you must seek information, you must ask open-ended questions, and most importantly, you must be approachable. You have to be someone that people want to talk to. Keep in mind that results do not come quickly. If you currently operate in a home where there isn't great communication, it will feel like an uphill battle at the beginning. Things will improve as communication improves, but you have to be consistent and patient. You have to understand things didn't get to where they are overnight, and they will not improve overnight.

They will improve over time as long as you stay consistent with your efforts around communication and creating an environment where it is valued. Success always favors consistency. A refusal to quit is a huge part of winning in any area, and communication is no exception. You need to show up every day with a plan that places communication at its center and make continuous efforts to improve your communication skills. This approach will produce favorable outcomes. It will never be easy, but with focused effort and aggressive patience, it will get better over time. It never becomes easy because, as you improve the communication among your team, you're going to continually have a desire to grow, and as a result, you will discover new challenges, which will be difficult for some time. Communication done correctly means the cycle of improvement never ends. As soon as things get a little bit easier, you will find a new opportunity, and your team will help you find a new area to focus on and a new challenge to solve. Then, it becomes difficult again until you collaboratively build a plan. You start to execute that plan, you're consistent, you're working at it every single day, and then it gets a little easier, and the process starts all over again; once again, there is no finish line.

Like all leadership skills, communication is perishable. We aren't born as great communicators. We aren't just given the skills required for communication. It is a skill that we have to develop and practice religiously. We must consistently work to improve communication because it has the unique ability to positively or negatively impact all other elements of leadership. Communication is critically important to overall satisfaction, fulfillment, and happiness among our staff. If you want to improve your ability to lead and increase the overall satisfaction of your team, focus on improving your ability to communicate effectively. Everything starts with the ability to identify, share, and solve problems together.

Communication is not only critical it is also incredibly complicated. We have attempted to share a few of our most effective communication strategies, in no way is this an exhaustive list. Our hope is that this chapter ignites your curiosity to seek more opportunities to practice your communication skills. This focus will allow you to discover your gifts and opportunities when it comes to effective communication. Be a curious communicator and discover new ways to connect with those that you lead.

Up until this point, we have focused on the team and the importance of giving your people 100% of you. The selfless leaders we have enjoyed working with in the healthcare field always try to put the team first. They put everyone's needs ahead of their own. The only problem with this noble approach is that when you are not focused on taking care of yourself, you will never be able to fully pour into your team. Your tank will never be full. Great leaders need to understand the importance and value of self-improvement—growing yourself so that you can more effectively grow your people. So let's get into our favorite subject: YOU!

A LEGACY Leader...

...Grows Themselves in Order to Grow Others

Most healthcare professionals are selfless by nature. They're often nurses or doctors or some other professional caregiver who is focused on the well-being of everyone else and places their needs above their own. Healthcare leaders are typically servant leaders who truly care about the success and well-being of everyone around them. Unfortunately, this is often at their own sacrifice. At home, they're focused on their family, their kids, their spouse, and then they get to work, and they're focused on their residents, their patients, their boss, their employees, and all of the people they work with throughout the day. We all have a finite amount of energy, and when we spend it all making everyone better, there isn't anything left to make ourselves better. But in order to be a strong leader, you have to focus on growing yourself. It is impossible for you to give 100% of yourself to the people you care the most about if you never have 100% to give.

Many times, we're focused on others and don't realize that we are not giving them everything that we could as a leader, a mom, a nurse, or any of those roles you fulfill. You're not able to complete those duties at the level that you would be able to if you were focused on yourself first. It is an uncomfortable concept for healthcare professionals to be selfish. But in order to allow you to fulfill your potential as a leader, you do have to be a little bit selfish. You have to be focused on yourself to be the best for others: those in your care, your patients, your residents, and your staff members.

To make this more palatable, you must start with a growth mindset. You have to understand that becoming a great leader starts with your own personal growth. Personal growth is liberating. As you begin to grow as a leader and prioritize yourself, you gain the ability to manage stress and focus on the elements that are within your control. With that mindset, you will start to view challenges as opportunities, and you will seek those opportunities to grow yourself.

Viewing challenges as opportunities is a powerful way to become better at anything and everything. You must be inspired by success, including that of others. Success has to be inspirational. Do not focus on jealousy, hatred, or negativity, or not understanding why someone else is experiencing success. You don't need to be distracted by that. You have to be focused on your own success and that of your team and those in your care. A growth mindset helps to direct our focus to the appropriate areas. You'll be able to focus on growing and advancing your skillset, whether as a leader or caregiver. Growing your skill set to become the best version of yourself so that you can give the most to others is a critical part of this growth mindset. We fully believe and respect the fact that we attract more of whatever we focus on. The Law of Attraction describes the relationship between humans and energy and the fact that we absolutely attract more of what our mind focuses on.

For example, when we focus on being upset that a competitor is experiencing success, the universe receives that as us not liking success and responds by keeping success from us. When we get caught up in the dangerous mindset of feeling defeated and focusing on all the reasons we can't win, our friendly universe sends us more of the stuff we are focusing on.

A big part of your growth will be dependent on your ability to accept constructive criticism and apply lessons learned. Things aren't going to always be smooth. You need to take constructive criticism from those you respect and from yourself as you reflect on opportunities and the challenges that you face. Extending grace and compassion to oneself makes it easier to accept and utilize your own criticism, which is different from negative self-talk. As humans, we are often more compassionate with others and forget that we need to extend ourselves the same level of grace.

Are you able to filter out negative talk but focus on constructive criticism so that you can grow as an individual through some self-coaching? Do you have a coach? Do you have somebody you can lean on who can help you grow as an individual? If not, you should identify someone who can help you grow. Maybe they're a level or two above where you are today, and they have some of the qualities you desire to have yourself. When you are evaluating a coach or even processing whether or not to take recommendations from someone, consider the source. Is this someone who has experienced success in the areas that you are trying to grow? Are they someone who is able to share experiences and the elements that made their success possible? Are they someone who has your best interest in mind, or are they simply trying to get paid? Find someone who has walked in your shoes, has had success, and is in a position to help you grow rather than simply looking to exploit you as a client of a program that may be unproven.

Have an open mind to the endless possibilities. You should not limit yourself as a leader. You can grow to any level you desire as long as you have an open mind and willingness to put in the work. The world is yours when you choose to focus on opportunities and be inspired by success. You will start to grow as an individual and as a leader and be more effective for those in your care.

Leaders will always value learning over recognition. We don't necessarily need to be recognized. Recognition will follow success; I assure you of that. But if you're focused on the recognition over the learning, you will always fall short of your potential. When you are able, focus on learning and acquiring new skills in order to make yourself the best version of you, growth occurs.

Through these activities and actions, the confidence you have in your ability to lead people will soar. You will become a confident leader who has a bucket capable of filling all buckets around you, and everyone around you will get better.

Many times, people in our care setting started careers in healthcare to care for people. They never looked at it as a path to becoming a leader. One day, someone asks you to take on a leadership role. Most of the time, this is a result of you being effective as a caregiver, operator, or sales professional, and someone sees that leadership potential in you. Now, you are in a leadership role, and you have the awesome opportunity to help others become great in the position you previously held, all with the goal of improving our care setting. This is where the most critical evolution of leadership happens. We have to understand that our ability to improve the skills of our team is the element that will improve our care setting. We are in charge of the individuals who will collectively impact post-acute care, so there is no job more important than developing yourself as a leader. It is acceptable to be a little bit selfish; the effectiveness of our care setting depends on it.

Many times, the idea of investing in you is stopped at the first excuse. The most common excuse for any change is that we do not have time. I experienced this myself and had to go through an activity that helped me make time.

We all have the same 24 hours in the day, yet there are so many different levels of achievement experienced in those 24 hours. During the same 24-hour period, some people accomplish so many things while others accomplish little to nothing. We don't all have the same resources, that is true, but what you choose to do with your 24 hours will help you to gain or to lose resources depending on the choices you make. In order for me to achieve my goals and not sacrifice my own personal development, I needed to create a 13th month for myself every year. I make it a priority to wake up one hour earlier than I used to and to go to bed one hour later. That effectively gives me two hours that I would otherwise have spent sleeping, watching television, or engaging in some other mindless activity that did not contribute to my personal goals. Adding those two hours every single day across the average 30-day month gives me 60 additional hours to focus on my goals, to work on things like writing this book, and investing in myself. When you take those 60 hours across the 12-month year, that creates an additional 720 hours. Divide 720 hours by a 24-hour day and—*boom!*—30 extra days each year! That gives me 30 full days, which is my 13th month. So, for every year, I get 13 months by waking up an hour early and going to bed an hour later, while my competition is working with only 12 months.

This discipline allows me to create distance. The most important part of this shift in time management is being fully committed to using those two hours to focus on growing myself, free of distractions, free of mindlessness. I try to be extremely purposeful with those 720 hours. This has made me a lot more productive, efficient, and effective. It has eliminated a ton of stress. It has given me time to focus on myself so that I can grow and achieve the things that I need to be satisfied in this life without having to sacrifice the other things I care about, like my wife, our children, their sports teams, or my friends.

Time is usually our number one excuse why we don't change. I had to shift my mindset and look at prioritizing my time. A framework that helped me do that is to view time as currency. I look at the minutes of the day the same way I do dollars in a bank account. I look at time as currency, and when that currency is spent, it's gone forever. As a result, I intensely scrutinize the things that I choose to spend my time on. I ask myself, *Is this something I would purchase? Is this something that I would spend my most precious resource on?* And if it's yes, then I invest, and I get excited because I know I am about to work my ass off to ensure I get a return on my investment. If I spend time doing an activity, if I spend time at an event, if I spend time reading a book or listening to a podcast, then I expect to get a return on that investment. I look at that time as well spent if it helps me grow or allows me to become a better leader so I can help someone else grow. If you would not spend money on it, don't waste your time on it. We can make more money; we cannot make more time. So, truly value your time over everything. And when you eliminate the things that are not contributing to your goals, you will discover that you have a tremendous amount of time that you weren't aware of. You can use that to invest in yourself, and you will get a return on the investment when you're focused on yourself. Time and money are like shit: If you leave it in a pile, it stinks, but when you spread it out, things grow. And when it comes to time, you are what grows!

Focusing on personal and professional development is necessary for a growth mindset. We have to seek learning opportunities. Creating extra time will allow you to do that. You will not find time; you have to make an active effort to create time. You must control your schedule in order to make time for the things that matter most. You also have to prioritize your physical and mental health to be the best version of *you.* Do things like move your body daily and simply be intentional with movements. A walk, a jog, yoga, stretching—anything to get your blood flowing a little bit throughout the day will benefit you immensely. Consume healthy things, whether that's food or beverages. Be more hydrated. Take care of yourself. Limit alcohol and toxins in your body. The more of these that you can remove, the better you're going to function, process things, learn new things, adapt to new challenges, and ultimately be happy. When you find happiness, you can experience tremendous growth as an individual. Your mind is your most powerful tool—use it!

Your thoughts control your words. Your words lead to actions, and those actions produce your outcomes. If you're unhappy with your current outcomes, you must fix your mind first. Your mind controls everything else. In order to improve your outcomes, you must start with your thoughts.

They're extremely powerful and can help you achieve fulfillment and happiness. You must take care of yourself to be able to provide value to others. Start with your mind. You must be selfish in order to be selfless. In order to be the giving person that you naturally are, to be the servant leader that you want to be, to be comfortable with continually giving to others, you must first focus on *you.*

When it comes to mental health, consume information that helps you grow. Try to avoid negative content altogether, especially things that are beyond your control. If you have no control over them, there's no reason to pay attention to them. Focus on reading books, listening to podcasts, attending seminars, attending healthcare association events, looking at leadership development opportunities for yourself—things that are going to help you grow. Again, when looking at leadership development or considering a personal coach or a mentor, use the filter of *Does this person have qualities that I want to have? Have they experienced levels of success that you desire?* There's no one better suited to teach you than somebody who has already walked the path. Now, you may not follow the same path, but you can learn valuable lessons that may save you time and resources along the way. Therefore, be intentional in understanding your mentor or coach—the person from whom you are trying to gain knowledge—and grow alongside them.

Another area where people struggle with investing in themselves is around the idea of setting boundaries. When you don't set boundaries effectively, people take advantage of your time and your desire to help others, and they will continue to pile things on your plate that will consume your time and ability to focus on yourself. Many of you may be living in that world today where you haven't appropriately set boundaries, and people have taken advantage of your kindness. This has created an environment where you are not able to focus on yourself. It's critically important to set and respect boundaries. You must value yourself, your time, and your goals enough to set boundaries. We've created a model, a **Hierarchy of Boundaries**, to help our team, our clients, our friends, complete strangers, and especially our readers to navigate the challenging waters of setting and helping others respect your boundaries. The levels of our pyramid are the following:

- **Communication**
- **Setting boundaries**
- **Self-understanding**
- **Mission alignment**
- **Defining priorities**
- **Creating an effective exit strategy**

As with any hierarchical model, you must satisfy each level before advancing to the next.

The base of our pyramid, as in most things, is communication. This is the foundation. This is where you must establish clear channels of communication between you, your leaders, your team members, and your subordinates so that you can effectively communicate your boundaries.

Then, at the second level, you have to create discipline by setting boundaries in all areas of your life. Like Nick Sabin, we believe that the way you do one thing is the way you do everything. So you must set boundaries at home. You must set boundaries with your personal development. You must set boundaries at work so that they can be respected and you can focus on the things that contribute to your goals.

The third level is self-understanding. You have to know yourself. Listen to yourself when something doesn't feel right. Clearly understand your workflow, your role, and your responsibilities, and be able to define success for yourself so that you can effectively eliminate distractions and anything that doesn't contribute to your success. You have to understand yourself to set boundaries effectively. Mission alignment falls under this level. Do you understand the mission of your organization? Does it resonate with you? Does it align with your purpose? Are you inspired to accomplish it? Once you get to this mission alignment phase, you have to understand if you are aligned with the mission of the organization.

Because if you are, then it's going to be easy to set boundaries. If you're not, you're going to feel like you're constantly being piled on and taken advantage of because it doesn't resonate with your purpose, and it's never going to feel comfortable. Your energy is never going to be aligned if you're not aligned with the mission. After you are aligned with the mission, then you have to define priorities. You have to let people know what your priorities are. You have to share what you are willing and not willing to accept. If it doesn't contribute to your priorities and goals, you need to eliminate it and force people to respect those boundaries by defining your priorities.

Then, finally, after you've gone through each level of this hierarchy, at the very top of the pyramid is creating an effective exit strategy. You have to ensure you're willing and able to exit a bad situation when your boundaries are not being respected. Do not fall victim to a negative relationship due to lack of planning. Having an effective exit strategy is empowering and freeing. You feel comfortable and confident setting boundaries, and if they are not respected, you will feel comfortable leaving and finding a situation where they will be respected.

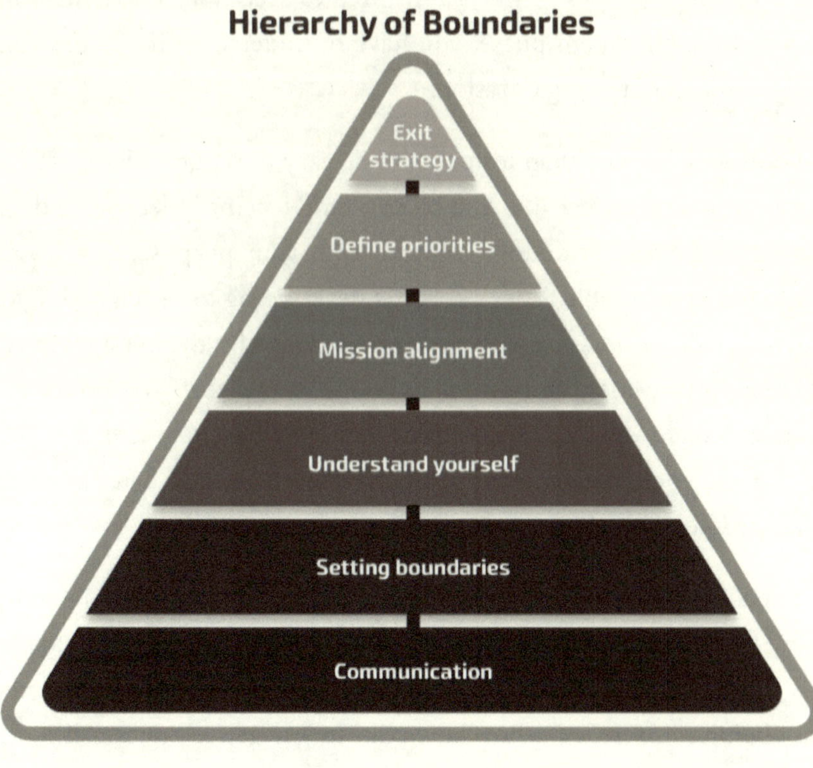

SCAN THE QR CODE To learn more about the hierarchy or experience the information in a different format. *Pillar Talk with Chris Ross*: Ep. 17 - "Hierarchy of Boundaries." (Spotify)

By focusing on yourself and growing as an individual, you will create the ability to be an invisible influence on those around you. If you're a parent, picture your children. If you are not a parent, think of yourself as a child. How well do kids listen to what their parents have to say? I know my children don't always listen to what I have to say, but our kids absolutely do pay attention to what we do. Your behaviors of focusing on yourself have the ability to influence those around you, whether it's your children, your spouse, your friends, your team members at work, or your subordinates. When people see you're focused on *you*, you're growing as an individual, and making yourself better physically and mentally through this self-development journey, they will respect that and pick up on some of those great qualities that you are producing by focusing on *you*.

Personally, I experienced this significantly during the several times I've completed the 75 Hard mental toughness recalibration program. People always seem to notice when I'm focused on myself, and it shows them that they are capable of doing those things too. They are capable of putting themselves first, moving their body, eliminating toxins, consuming things and information that are going to make them better, and setting effective boundaries so that other people will not take advantage of them. The right people will be inspired by seeing you win. You're showing them what they are capable of, and people who respect you will be inspired to do the same. You're showing them what is possible when they make the decision to invest in themselves and take action. As a leader, you have the ability and responsibility to inspire and influence your people. You can change somebody without saying a single word just by generating inspiration through action. Don't take this responsibility lightly.

Accomplished entrepreneur, world-renowned keynote speaker, and best-selling author Ed Mylett says, "You're the most qualified to help the person that you used to be." Think about the struggles you had when you were first starting out, or the struggles you had when you first got into leadership, or maybe something you're dealing with now. The person you are most qualified to assist is the person that you used to be. The position you previously held, the challenges you have successfully navigated, you're the most qualified to help that person. The person who has experienced what you're dealing with today is the most qualified to help you. Find somebody who understands, has walked in your shoes, understands your challenges, and can help you navigate the challenging waters of leadership.

Think of yourself. Who are you willing to follow? Think of your favorite leader, the person who grew you the most throughout your career. What were their key qualities? How many of those do you exemplify daily? What qualities did you value about them as a leader? What types of behaviors did they exhibit? Are you exhibiting those for your team? Are you somebody that you would follow?

Now, on the opposite end of the spectrum, think of your most frustrating boss or manager. What were their qualities? What are you doing to avoid those same pitfalls? Most people don't wake up desiring to be a bad manager or a bad boss. But if you go through the motions without being mindful or purposeful in your actions, you may end up adopting those same qualities and experiencing those same pitfalls. Are you taking an active approach to growing yourself as a leader? It can't be passive. Again, it's a perishable skill that you must focus on and practice in order to grow.

You must grow as a leader. To grow as a leader, you have to grow as an individual and be focused on yourself and your personal growth so that you have more to give to those in your care. Are you working hard every day to become a leader worth following?

One more important thing to understand when it comes to personal growth is that, like many things in life, there are ups and downs. You will experience peaks and valleys. There will be many times when you become stuck, or you feel as though you are not making progress fast enough. The especially frustrating times are when it appears everyone is growing except you. I assure you that is never the case. There are going to be times in your journey when you do not feel like doing the things you know are necessary for personal growth. You are going to get tired, frustrated, and simply fall off track because you lose motivation. Motivation will fade, and that is when discipline is necessary. Discipline is the ultimate separator between winners and losers. Winners figure out a way to get things done when motivation is absent. Losers make excuses.

A framework that I have used to help me get unstuck and back on track quickly when I fall off is our **3 A's of Getting Unstuck**.

1. **Awareness:** You must be aware of the situation and recognize that you are falling off track, not completing the tasks necessary to grow as an individual or as a leader. You have to be mindful of your daily actions and pay attention to the outcomes those actions are producing. Awareness is key because we are all going to stumble. We will all lose steam and slow down. But the people who figure out how to win big are those who can catch themselves early on in the stumble and course correct. The more aware you are, the quicker you can lean into your discipline to make up for lack of motivation.

2. **Assess:** It is then necessary to assess a time in your life when you were winning, everything was going smoothly, and you were growing. We have all experienced some level of success in at least one area of our lives. You need to spend some time reflecting on that time in your life and take inventory of your actions. What were you doing or not doing that caused you to be successful? Who were you

spending your time with? What were you spending your time doing? This assessment will give you the playbook of the items you were doing when you were winning and help you to identify which of those elements are missing. This assessment will help you to understand your personal recipe for success. It is different for each of us, so your honest assessment is critical to getting unstuck.

3. **Action:** Finally, and most importantly, it is time for action. Awareness is key; assessments are necessary, but both are useless without action! As soon as you recognize that your motivation is slipping (awareness) and you know which elements of your life are not in line with your goals (assessment), then you need to get to work to make the necessary changes (action). The greatest plans in the world are absolutely worthless without action. You have to do the work. There is no one coming to help or save you; your growth is dependent on you, so let's get to work!

Great leaders inspire and create an amazing culture. As a leader, the ultimate measurement of success is the culture you are able to create for your team. You want to create an environment that attracts and retains top talent. This is only possible with a strong growth-focused culture, which we discuss in the next chapter.

SCAN THE QR CODE To hear more about the "3 A's." *Pillar Talk with Chris Ross*: Ep. 31 - "Getting Unstuck" (Spotify)

A LEGACY Leader...

...Positively Impacts Culture

It was 2016, and the West Division was responsible for over 50 buildings across the western part of the United States. Over time, we were able to create a culture of growth and winning by investing in our people and pushing them beyond their comfort zones while challenging and supporting one another as leaders. We eventually became the most successful division in the organization in terms of census and revenue. As a result, we were given the responsibility to take over the support of ten additional facilities that were struggling in the Midwest. These homes were previously supported by a team that viewed themselves as consultants who simply provided recommendations but not actual support or implementation of effective strategies. They simply oversaw the facilities, visiting when needed or requested to provide feedback. Then, they allowed the teams to sort through what was important and valuable and decide how and when to implement different strategies. Not surprisingly, the outcomes were poor.

Census and revenue were at the bottom of the entire organization. Leadership was weak, and the homes were disconnected. As we took over the support of these centers, we identified key leaders. We spent time with them in their homes. We learned their challenges. We also helped them navigate the challenging environment of the post-acute care setting. I think one of the most important parts of this evolution is that we leaned into the local leadership teams to learn about them, their teams, their homes, and their markets. We were outsiders. Very few of us had ever operated or supported homes in the Midwest, and we had a lot to learn. We built credibility with the team by asking questions and listening to responses.

We showed them how to win, and we celebrated alongside them. Within a year, these homes successfully integrated and became a big part of the most successful division in the organization. They adapted to our culture of winning, and they started to perform well beyond previous limitations. They even reached a point of success where the previous support team had requested to have them back in their portfolio of responsibility. We politely declined and continued to win. Our winning culture was the catalyst that changed everything.

As we shift our thoughts to culture, I want you to imagine that you have one employee remaining in your organization, in your home, on your team. You have one employee remaining, but all responsibilities have remained the same. Workload, productivity, budget, census—all expectations stay the same. Now imagine that all methods of advertisement have been eliminated from your recruiting toolbox, except word of mouth. You're not able to use digital advertising, you're not able to take out an ad in the newspaper, you're not able to post anything on social media, and no holding signs up on a busy street corner. Your only way to get an additional employee is a word-of-mouth campaign, and that campaign must be started by that last remaining employee.

Now ask yourself, *How are you going to treat that person? What are you going to do to ensure they stay and help you fill those positions? What are you going to do for them to ensure that they go out and tell everybody how great you are and how wonderful it is to work at your organization?* The answer that you just told yourself is the answer for culture and leadership. Why wait until you have one employee? Why not treat every employee this way from day one? Leadership has a profound effect on the culture of an organization. It can help eliminate employee burnout and significantly reduce turnover. A strong culture will lead to individual and organizational growth. The absence of a strong culture will destroy the organization and the individuals that comprise it.

As we've discussed, people are our most important and valuable resource, and your people are the most important element of culture. We must focus on our people and on being the absolute best. When you focus on being the best and accepting nothing less in terms of people and culture, positive results follow. Results always follow the best people. However, people confuse this relationship and believe that the results are what makes someone the best. In reality, the best people create the best results. It starts with the people. You have to start with your people and invest in them. Results always follow the best people.

When you apply this approach to people and culture, you will begin to win and change the fabric of your organization. With people, we believe it's important to start every day with a win. The first thing that you talk about has to be positive. Many times in a home, we talk about all the negative things that occurred the night before or over the weekend. We talk about injuries or falls, missed medications, or "call-offs" with staff. We discuss all the challenges, the adverse things that occurred, and then we tell everybody to have a great day. If we want our people to have a great day, we have to start with a win and focus on the good. Managers frequently make the mistake of thinking culture is a passive byproduct of their leadership. In order for leaders to ensure that culture is top of mind for the team, we have to make it part of the conversation. Creating a strong culture takes active effort, and there is nothing passive about it. You have to keep the team engaged and focused on the progress that they're making. We can't simply focus on the pitfalls, or we'll get more of that.

One key element of culture is deleting the inessential tasks. If it doesn't contribute to being the best, you should delete it. You have to help your people understand the *why* behind each task you're asking them to complete on a daily basis. If you can't explain *why* it is important, then it should be eliminated, or you need to go to your supervisor and learn *why* the task is required. You will create an enormous amount of credibility with your team if you can a) help remove items from their plate that are not necessary or b) help them understand *why* each task is necessary. If they understand the *why*, they will likely be more committed to the mission. Your job as a leader when it comes to culture is to act like a surgeon—remove the things that are taking away from their focus on being the best.

There's a great Latin word that helps us understand this: *decidere*, the Latin word from which "decision" is derived. If you break down the two parts of the word, *de* means "off," and *cidere* means "to cut." Think of an incision. As we referenced before, you get to cut away the path you do not believe is necessary. The beauty of this approach is that, as a leader, you do get to decide. It's your direction that will help guide the team down the path of building a stronger culture. Many managers put culture on the back burner in order to focus on the status of the product, home, quality, or the organization. Many times, we're focused on all of the things that are measured by a typical organization—census, revenue, cash, state survey outcomes, and star ratings. There are very few organizations that focus on culture measurement because it is something that's difficult to measure. So, you have to shift your mind from focusing on the product and understand that the product will improve as the culture improves.

There are some homes that are in a very dark place today from a quality and product standpoint. We have to remind ourselves and our people that each new day starts in the dark, and yet the sun does come up. The only way to minimize the dark times is by building a team upon the foundation culture and creating a belief that they can overcome any obstacle—together.

Your team must understand that adversity introduces us to our true selves. Humans do not learn much when things are easy. We learn our greatest lessons through our biggest challenges and most difficult times. Culture is a great example of how we're able to learn through a struggle and come out better on the other side.

To assess where you are today, you have to be extremely honest with yourself when it comes to culture. You can't excuse away the results. You have to assess your current state, accept it, and put a plan together to move forward. Ask yourself, *What is our current culture?* During this exercise, your ego becomes your enemy. It's going to tell you things are better than they are. It's going to give you excuses for the way things are. It's going to allow you to believe it's not your fault. You have to ignore all that and accept the facts. As the leader of your team, you have to own it so that you can disarm it and do something about it.

You have to do the work. There are no shortcuts, no magic wands.

As we started to dive into culture more deeply, we wanted to learn and study the elements of culture ourselves. We wanted to define a process that would help people understand what the elements of a strong culture are, and how to implement those successfully in the post-acute care setting. In order to gain a better understanding of the elements necessary to build and grow a strong culture, we surveyed a large number of successful post-acute leaders across the country. These leaders are at various levels, but they all have a strong track record of creating or being part of strong cultures that produce winning teams with high retention rates, high employee satisfaction, and high employee engagement. As we collected their answers, five traits emerged as the most common and most important elements to build a strong culture that allows for growth, inspiration, and overall satisfaction among employees. Through this, we developed our **Culture Task List**. This approach was inspired by Andy Frisella and his Power List. Andy's Power List provides you with a simple yet powerful tool that will place intentional focus on critical, non-routine tasks that contribute to your goals. When we do not consistently place intentional focus on critical tasks, we fail.

Our Culture Task List will force you to focus on the process instead of becoming fixated on the outcome. At the beginning of this journey, the outcome of a strong and healthy culture in an organization may seem like a daunting task. But when you intentionally focus on the daily tasks that will lead you there, it will become more manageable and more satisfying. When we simply focus on the outcome, it feels like we're never making progress, and the goal seems impossible. As we developed our Culture Task List, we had to create a place to document our journey. Documentation allows us to create a book of reference to review progress and keep track of wins so that we can celebrate along the way, not simply at the end.

These were the five traits that emerged across the leaders that we surveyed to build a strong culture:

- **Trust**
- **Communication**
- **Building strong relationships with staff members**
- **Learn something new**
- **Celebrate wins & Having fun!**

As we converted Andy's Power List concept into Legacy's Culture Task List, we applied similar rules. Every single day, without fail, you must complete all five tasks in order to win the day. If you miss any of them, you lose the day and have to start over. Your goal is to stack as many wins as possible and as many days where you complete every task as possible.

The other element of the Task List is that you must document your journey for reference and to celebrate your victories. You can download it for free at our website qualitylhc.com, or by scanning the QR code at the end of this book. You can also document your journey in a notebook.

You can be flexible in what you do to satisfy each element, but you can't be flexible with the elements. You cannot replace trust or communication, but what you do to build trust or improve communication is completely up to you and your team. So every day, without fail, in order to stack a win, you must do something to build trust, something to create or practice clear communication, something to build or improve relationships with a staff member, you must attempt to learn something new, you must celebrate a win, regardless of how small, and you must have some fun. I highly recommend that you start the day with that celebration and set the tone for the day. Making work fun can be challenging in post-acute care, as we often deal with stressful situations, including death. This reality makes it critically important that we make the experience fun for our employees, our residents, and families.

The free download of our Task List is a small gift to you. If you would like to hear more about the Legacy CTL, you can check out Episode 9 of our podcast *Pillar Talk with Chris Ross*, "Culture Task List." We are confident that it will help you refine the leadership tactics you have learned throughout the book and start applying them toward building a culture that creates an environment where employees feel empowered, engaged, and energized. All these characteristics will lead to higher retention, higher satisfaction, and higher employee engagement, which will ultimately help you achieve all of the business goals you have set for yourself.

We hope you found the framework, mindset, tools, and stories in this book helpful. The most important element of sharing our journey with you is that it is intended to inspire action. The lessons shared cannot remain within the pages of this book if they are going to make a difference. Our mission is to **Improve Quality Through Collaboration**, and the only way we can accomplish this on a large enough scale and make a positive difference is with you!

Action is your responsibility as a leader, but now you are part of the Legacy family, so let's get to work together!

Conclusion

At this point in our journey, I hope that we can all agree that the solution to all of the challenges that we face on a daily basis starts with us. As we individually choose to improve ourselves and those around us, our entire care setting will collectively improve. The most exciting part about leadership is that it's 100% within your control. Every day, you have the opportunity to choose to improve in the key areas we have discussed. As covered throughout the book, there is no magic wand, and no one is coming to help. The work is never going to get easy, and there's no finish line, but it is necessary and absolutely worth it. There are not many things more rewarding or satisfying in life than leadership done right. You have the ability to change your world and the world of those around you.

Now that you have made the choice to embark on this journey, not only do you have new tools, knowledge, and opportunities, but you also have the responsibility to grow your people, grow yourself, and grow our care setting. Do not wish for things to be easy. Prepare for the difficulties of leadership. The irony is that when we prepare for a difficult journey, things do become easier. It certainly does not work the other way around.

Enjoy the process because that is where all the growth happens. The process is the destination, as you will never be done leading. Progress follows those who can commit to consistency with the process, even when results appear to be invisible.

I'd like you to think of a piñata for a minute. When you're at a party, they bring out a piñata, and people start swinging at it. You don't notice the damage after the first number of hits, but with each strike, it becomes weaker, and then towards the end, each hit appears to have a much larger impact, and finally, one last blow splits it apart, sending treats to everyone at the party. We understand that the treats were not a result of the final blow but rather a result of the collective effort of the group. Leadership works in a similar fashion. It takes a group effort, and at the beginning, each task seems like it takes a great deal of effort with little measurable outcome. But as you remain consistent, each task will have a greater result, and, eventually, we will all receive treats in the forms of growth, fulfillment, and happiness.

Thank you for taking the time to invest in yourself and, by extension, in your people. I genuinely value time above all forms of currency. We have no idea how much we get, and when it's gone, there is no restart button. The only things that will remain are the outcomes we are able to produce with the time we are given—our *Legacy*.

So thank you for choosing to spend some of your most valuable resource with us. Our biggest hope is that you will find a significant return on your investment.

To reiterate, our mission is to **Improve Quality Through Collaboration**, and we look forward to hearing about your wins. Now that you are part of the Legacy leadership family, we are cheering for you. I wanted to write this book because of the countless gaps I've experienced and witnessed in post-acute leadership. Most of the time, the shortcomings are due to a lack of knowledge and/or experience. I hope that we were able to effectively share our knowledge and relevant experiences with you so that your journey may be a little more rewarding.

Everything you desire exists on the other side of discipline. If you commit to growing yourself and your people, you will win. Become relentlessly committed to achieving your true potential as a leader. The effort will be worth it. Leadership is hard, but so is having no one to lead in a dysfunctional work environment. Both paths require a tremendous amount of effort on your part, but one is significantly more satisfying. Choose your hard.

Our journey together is coming to an end—or, hopefully, just a pause until we are able to collaborate. Please understand that reading this book will only be worth the time you spent when you apply the lessons learned. The contents cannot remain between the covers. The foundation has been laid. Now, it is your responsibility to build on it. Leadership is the first step and one of the most critical to our success and sustainability as a care setting. As we become great leaders, it's our responsibility to improve the culture of the organizations we operate. Leaders have the ability to change their environment.

Stay connected with us on social media and listen to us on *Pillar Talk with Chris Ross* to learn how we plan to positively impact the culture of the post-acute care setting, one home at a time. We hope to collaborate with each of you in the near future.

Let's freaking GROW!!

THANK YOU FOR READING MY BOOK!

DOWNLOAD YOUR FREE GIFTS

Just to say thanks for buying and reading my book, I would like to give you a few free bonus gifts, no strings attached!

Scan the QR Code:

I appreciate your interest in my book, and value your feedback as it helps me improve future versions of this book. I would appreciate it if you could leave your invaluable review on Amazon.com with your feedback. Thank you!

www.ingramcontent.com/pod-product-compliance
Lightning Source LLC
LaVergne TN
LVHW051011080826
845145LV00009B/2574